The Embossed Tea Kettle

Orate Gama
and other works

Hakuin Zenji

Translated from the Japanese
by R.D.M. Shaw, D.D.

This edition abridged and revised by Diana St Ruth.

Buddhist Publishing Group
Totnes

The Embossed Tea Kettle

Orate Gama
and other works of

Hakuin Zenji

the Zen reformer of the eighteenth century in Japan

The mystic words *O Ra Te* seem to
have been embossed on Hakuin's tea
kettle. He faced them daily as he
meditated and wrote. He chose them
as the title of his principal popular work.

Translated from the Japanese
by R.D.M. Shaw, D.D.

This edition abridged and revised by Diana St Ruth.

Buddhist Publishing Group
Totnes

Buddhist Publishing Group
Totnes, England

www.buddhistpublishing.com
www.buddhismnow.com

ISBN 9780946672332

First published by George Allen & Unwin Ltd, 1963

Diana St Ruth asserts the moral right to be identified as the editor of this work.

A catalogue record for this book is available from the British Library.

Contents

Illustrations

Editor's Note

Dr R.D.M. Shaw was a Christian missionary brought up in Japan. He, perhaps understandably, took great interest in the Japanese forms of Buddhism, and translated several texts into English, texts which had never been translated before. This he did with the encouragement of his Japanese Christian and Buddhist friends including Dr D.T. Suzuki, a scholar of note who contributed substantially to the understanding of Buddhism in Western countries, and Mr Christmas Humphreys who co-founded the Buddhist Society, London in 1924, an organisation which exists to this day and is one of the oldest outside Asia.

This translation of Hakuin's writings was originally published in 1963 by George Allen & Unwin. It quickly became a classic amongst Buddhist practitioners of the time. Since then much interest has developed in Buddhism and many books have appeared on the shelves of ordinary bookshops, in contrast to the one or two prior to the 1960s. Quite a number of the ancient texts had been translated into English years earlier, some by Christian missionaries living in the East. In recent years many of these old and ancient texts have been translated again, including most of this one which has been out of print for some considerable time.

Hakuin has come under some criticism by modern scholars for making 'mistakes' in names and dates, for repeating stories, and doing so 'inaccurately'. But just think, here was a man experiencing the dharma there and then; he was seeing it and being it. He was not remembering a story from a scholastic or historic perspective, but simply putting across a particular point to ordinary people. He also sometimes used names and dates which were not entirely accurate according to previous works — again, much like anyone might do without reference to those works.

If some of Hakuin's remarks seem meaningless to us because we don't know the background to them, we can simply pass them by. There is no doubt, however, that the underlying message throughout this volume is entirely consistent.

I do not think for one minute that Dr Shaw undertook this task for any other purpose than to experience for himself the Zen of Hakuin. His turn of phrase undoubtedly caught Hakuin's sense of humour and irony. It was, therefore, my honour and privilege to undertake editing this book which was rather like brushing away a few cobwebs on Dr Shaw's half a century old manuscript. My intention was to straighten out some awkward sentences, and yet to maintain their original meaning. I hope I have to a degree achieved this.

Finally, I wish to thank my husband, Richard, for his help throughout this endeavour, and James Whelan, a Buddhist practitioner and linguist, who went through the manuscript with a fine-tooth comb, picking up obvious errors and making invaluable suggestions.

I hope readers enjoy this book as much as I have.

Diana St Ruth
Totnes 2021

Foreword

by Dr David Friedman

In respect of the current impact of Zen on the West, it has been said that never before have so many evinced such interest in anything so little understood.[i] However, these many occidental Zen devotees are perhaps not altogether to blame for their ignorance. For this Chinese-Japanese 'ultra-self-power wing of Buddhism', as it has been called,[ii] is actuated by a paradoxical doctrine, essentially simple, yet difficult to grasp. By its very nature, it eludes clear-cut definitions. For it seems that in order to attain its central goal, *satori* (enlightenment), or intuitional awakening, it must be lived and not read. Every attempt, therefore, to communicate this spiritual experience coherently in writing or speech must necessarily miscarry.

Such an approach to religion and philosophy is perhaps not immediately congenial to the Western mind. According to Professor Daisetz Teitaro Suzuki, Zen is altogether beyond the ken of human understanding. Its uniqueness lies in its irrationality, its passing beyond logical comprehension. The normal rationalistic common sense view of things has apparently no use in evaluating its truth or untruth.[iii] And, indeed, its difficulty lies perhaps in the intellectual inability to transcend the intellect which, according

i *The Essentials of Zen Buddhism*. An Anthology of the Writings of D.T. Suzuki, edited, with an introduction by Bernard Phillips, London, 1963.

ii D.T. Suzuki, *Essays in Zen Buddhism*, First Series, Buddhist Society edition, London, 1963.

iii id. *Living by Zen*, Tokyo, 1949.

to Zen, is a prerequisite for the realisation of absolute reality in one's own life. In the wake of Indian Mahayana Buddhism, Zen draws radical conclusions from the fundamental doctrine that there is no 'essential' difference between the absolute and phenomenal (empirical) reality (nirvana and samsara), or in other words, they are neither identical nor different. If the former transcends the categories of space, time and discursive thought — and thus is impredicable and inexpressible — this must, in essence, hold for the latter too.

Hence, in terms of its transmission, the problem of Zen is the expression of the inexpressible, which can be better achieved by the suggestive power of art than by philosophical statements. On the other hand, inasmuch as nirvana is identical with buddhahood, all beings are primordially endowed with buddha-nature, entailing absolute freedom. Owing to the limitations of mere rational thought, we fail to realise this in ourselves.

Zen, therefore, is the way from bondage to freedom. It is the art of seeing into the nature of one's own being by penetrating into the very depths of inner spiritual truth. This is the object of Zen discipline with its enigmatic, seemingly paradoxical unsolvable-problems-to-be-solved *(koan)*, its equally enigmatic dialogues *(mondo)*, its sessions of concentrated meditation *(zazen)*, and its frequently painful 'shock-treatments' inflicted by the masters upon argumentative disciples.

Zen is neither an escapist nor a nihilistic doctrine. Rather, it aims at transforming life into a work of art, as it were. The paradoxical koans are attempts to liberate the spirit from petrified norms so as to revalue all conventional contradictory ideas such as affirmation and negation, right and wrong, truth and falsehood, beauty and ugliness, on a higher spiritual plane. This can be achieved only through transcendent wisdom *(prajna)*, which is not merely knowledge and understanding but the highest power of intuition.

By the realisation of enlightenment 'suddenly' revealed after a long assiduous training, the inner essence of all things is grasped, leading to a harmonious communion with the transcendent beauty of nature, as suggested in many Zen paintings. *Satori* removes the barriers of the mind from the inmost self, thus releasing and purifying all the natural energies, and all the potentially creative and benevolent impulses. As a method, Zen is based on the practice of intense self-discipline and the cultivation of such virtues as courage, perseverance, clear insight and compassion. Its ultimate aim is perfect spiritual transfiguration, bringing about a new dynamic view of life and the universe which — *'sub specie aeternitatis'* — rather than negating, illumines the multiplex and multiform empirical world of subject and object. When this is attained, the inner truth is said to suffuse completely everyday thought and action in such a way that all possible occurrences, great and small, joyful and calamitous, can be met.

Zen, therefore, has a great practical value. 'No work, no food' was an established rule for the Zen monk. It has certainly left its mark on painting, literature, temple architecture, fencing, archery, the tea ceremony, and — during certain periods — on the socio-political situation of Japan.

Suzuki's 'irrational' interpretation of Zen, indicating that it is 'above space-time relations and naturally above historical facts' is not accepted by all scholars in the field.[iv] Rather, they maintain that it forms an integral part of the history of Chinese as well as Japanese thought and, therefore, must be understood in its proper historical setting.

---

iv See e.g. Hu Shih, *Chan (Zen) Buddhism in China, its History and Method, Philosophy East and West,* volume 3, Honolulu, 1953, pp. 3-24 and D.T.S., A Reply to Hu Shih, id. pp. 25-46.

The pros and cons of these two attitudes cannot be discussed in a short foreword, but the historical approach, in addition to the spiritual, is certainly relevant to the interesting career of Hakuin himself, as will be seen from the selection of his many writings given here in a lucid English translation.

The two oldest and most important Zen sects are the Rinzai and Soto, each of which has its own hierarchy and line of patriarchs. Although they have similar aims and doctrines, they differ in their methods. As stated by Reiho Masunaga (in *The Soto Approach to Zen,* Tokyo, 1958), Zen is not mysticism. Soto rejects the use of the baffling koans and accepts logic and science as well as the reading and teaching of the Buddhist scriptures, even if not as the final authority. It emphasises the relation between wisdom and compassion. Helping others seems to count more in Soto than in Rinzai. Whereas there was a close association of Rinzai with the 'reigning families', Dogen who brought Soto from China to Japan in 1228, preferred ordinary people. For the later period, these hard and fast distinctions are not borne out by the life and works of Hakuin (1685-1769) who averted the decline of the Rinzai movement and became the founder of modern Zen.

Hakuin was a man of extraordinary gifts, mystic and practical, strong and gentle, imbued with true compassion and with an open eye for the miseries of the human situation on all levels. Moreover, he was a great painter — unique among the artists of his time[v] — as well as a prolific writer with an acute power of (realistic) observation, yet 'attuned to the silent music that accompanies every manifestation of life'.[vi] Even though he is regarded by the

v See the admirable publication on Zen painting, written in German by Kurt Brasch, *Hakuin und die Zen-Malerei*, Tokya, 1957.

vi Osvald Siren. *The Chinese on the Art of Painting*, quoted in 6, p. 11. See also Heinrich Dumoulin, *A History of Zen Buddhism*, London 1963, which contains a long chapter on Hakuin.

Japanese themselves as the great outstanding figure of the later Zen period, only incidental passages from his works have been given in English translation by Suzuki and other scholars. Hakuin tried to express difficult Zen sayings (koan) in a vigorous colloquial language accessible to all. Apart from their spiritual value, his works are full of human interest, shedding light on the contemporary political, social and customary situation of Japan.

Dr Shaw's lively and well-written translations, therefore, will certainly appeal to all those interested in Zen, not only as a spiritual discipline, but also as an inspiring cultural force.

D. Friedman

[Dr David Friedman (1903-1984) was born in Amsterdam. At an early age he took a keen interest in Buddhism and became a noted lecturer, reader and professor over a period of time at some of the great universities of the world. In 1950 he taught at the University of London's School of Oriental and African Studies and by doing so joined a distinguished group of European Orientalists who took part in the post-war expansion of Oriental studies in Britain. (Editor)]

Author's Note

It is a great many years since my attention was drawn to the works of Hakuin Zenji. For many years I was a missionary living in the near neighbourhood of Hakuin's temple, Shoin-ji. It was also my privilege to have the acquaintance of the late revered Dr Takakusu. One summer Dr Takakusu was lecturing at a Retreat House for Young Buddhists, which he had established nearby on the slopes of Mount Fuji. One day I visited him there, and in response to a question, he suggested that I might like to introduce the works of Hakuin Zenji to the West. So it is to him that this book may be said to owe its origin.

Several Japanese Christian friends gave me their help. One of them chose the editions of Hakuin's works which have been used. It is a Japanese Christian lady in collaboration with the abbot of a Zen temple in Tokyo, who took much trouble in obtaining for me the illustrations.

These illustrations serve to show that there is a whole aspect of Hakuin's character which I have not been able to deal with in this book. Hakuin was an artist as well as a poet and religious leader.

I also want to thank Dr Daisetz Suzuki who gave me encouragement and advice, as well as Dr David Friedman for his kindness in writing the foreword. Finally, I would like to express my thanks to my wife for her help in the preparation of the text. The author alone, however, is responsible for any remaining faults.

A Short Life of Hakuin

Hakuin was born on 25 December 1685. His father's family name had been Sugiyama, but after being adopted into his wife's family at the time of their marriage, it was changed to Nagasawa. His mother was the daughter of the postmaster of the town of Hara in the province of Suruga.

The Nagasawa family belonged to the Nichiren sect, and this was of importance in the spiritual development of the son, Iwajiro (Hakuin).

From his earliest years Iwajiro was noted for his remarkable memory. It is said that at the age of four he could repeat by heart over three hundred village songs, and that once after returning from a service where a sermon had been preached on the Devadatta Chapter of the *Saddharma Pundarika Sutra (Hokke-kyo)*, he astonished everybody by giving them an accurate account of all that he had heard.

Unfortunately, a sermon on the eight hot hells which he once heard, terrified him, and it was a long time before he recovered from the spiritual shock. Eventually, however, as a result of his terror, he was moved to seek for the truth. He had difficulty in persuading his parents to permit him to leave home and begin a serious religious life by entering a temple and accepting the guidance of a priest. The temple was Shoin-ji, of the Rinzai School of Zen. At last, on 26 March 1699, he received primary ordination at the hands of Tan Reiden. Iwajiro's name was then changed to Ekaku.

From that day he began his long religious quest. He went from one temple to another, from one famous priest to another. The search was interrupted for a time by the death of his mother in 1706, but he continued studying the scriptures *(The Kokoshu, a Collection of Lectures for Zen Retreats)* and the *(Shijunisho-kyo, The Sutra of the Forty-Two Chapters)*. At one time he was much influenced by the famous poet Bao, who lived in Zuiun-ji in the province of Mino. Hakuin's clear and polished literary style was no doubt due in great measure to the influence of this poet.

In 1708 he went to study at a temple in Takata in the province of Echigo, under a priest named Shotetsu, after which he moved to Iiyama in the province of Shinano, and studied under an old priest named Etan of Shoju-an. This old priest treated Hakuin in an offhand and rough manner. Most young men would have taken offence and gone off to more congenial surroundings, but Hakuin was deeply impressed by the old man's character, and patiently bore the harsh treatment he received. After many months 'under the hammer and shackles' of this teacher, he was rewarded for his patience.

'One morning,' said Hakuin, 'as I wandered alone round the town of Iiyama on my customary alms round, a wonderful idea came into my mind, of which I could not rid myself. I became so obsessed with this idea, that I did not notice where my feet carried me. Suddenly I found myself, without knowing how I had come there, at the door of someone's house begging alms. For a long time I stood there absorbed in this new idea. The master of the house who had ordered me to go away over and over again, finally took up a writing brush and hurled it at me.'

Hakuin's face was cut and he was knocked over in a faint. The neighbours rushed out to see what had happened, but the bustle and noise did not penetrate into his mind. His whole being was still filled with the great thought. Two or three passers-by lifted him up and asked him what the matter was, but he clapped his hands and burst out laughing. Everybody who saw this, thought he was just a crazy priest and went on their way. After Hakuin had come to himself, he brushed off the mud and dust from his clothes and returned to his temple with a smiling face. As he reached the temple, his teacher, Etan, who was standing on the verandah and saw him coming, called out: 'Something has happened to you! What is it?' Hakuin related the whole morning's experience and what his great thought had been. His old teacher said: 'Now you must take the vows and not be satisfied with that attainment. From now on your studies need to be deeper than ever. Your life will be more strenuous since this enlightenment has come to you.'

Etan Shoju's long continued discipline had at last produced its effect. Hakuin had grasped the inexpressible reality of the nature of mind. He had reached enlightenment, knowledge of the nature of truth.

Soon after this experience, Hakuin was called back to nurse his first teacher at Daisho-ji in Numazu, near his old home in Hara. It was here at temples in the neighbourhood that he studied the *Pi-yen lu (Hekiganroku*, or *Blue Cliff Records*), the *Diamond Sutra*, and many other great scriptures.

Now, however, his own health began to deteriorate. His account of his illness and his remarkable recovery is given in the *Yasen Kanna*.

After his recovery, Hakuin continued his studies and also continued travelling widely, seeking further wisdom from well-known teachers in all parts of the country. Sometimes he was tempted into staying with enlightened priests, no matter how cold and uncomfortable the place might be, and he expressed his feelings in two short poems:

> Oh! let me hear again the echo of that snow, falling
>   in the twilight
> at that ancient temple in the grove of Shinoda!

And one which is a sort of motto for his life:

> Having heard the Way in the evening
>   let me die in the morning.

After still further pilgrimages, he had intended to retire to a distant hermitage in the province of Mino (to a place called Iwataki), but was dissuaded from doing so by an urgent message from his father who was on the point of dying. He therefore returned home. After his father's death, he took up residence at Shoin-ji which was desolate and almost derelict. It was here that he had begun his religious life, and here he lived in great poverty until the end of his days, only going away when requested to lecture and teach at temples, mostly in the near neighbourhood.

His piety and learning soon became known throughout the land. Many great persons and hundreds of young students came to him for guidance and instruction. How spiritually contented he was, in spite of his many material discomforts, is shown by this little poem he composed at the time:

> Feelings of pity and harshness
>   all are reduced by distance
> Happy indeed, I will not seek
>   the hills of any distant country.

Here in his first and last temple Hakuin died at the age of eighty-four, on 18 January 1769. The posthumous title of Shinki Dokumyo was bestowed upon him soon afterwards.

Hakuin Zenji and his Peasant Parishioners

One of the delightful traits of Hakuin Zenji's character was his affection for his poorer parishioners. His knowledge of their circumstances and their states of mind came partly from this affection for them, and partly from the fact that he also had experienced deep poverty.

The faulty policies of the Tokugawa shogunal authorities were now producing their effects. These effects were being felt in the life of the nation as a whole, as well as in the religious life of the temples. Perhaps the chief of these policies was the attempt to perpetuate the class or caste system of feudalism, keeping their own family and their own immediate feudatory families, not only as the topmost class, but as a prosperous and wealthy class.

The enforced residence of the provincial nobles and their families in Yedo for months at a time, had not only increased the size of that city, but had led to an increase in luxurious living and much dissipation. Though two or three of the Shoguns fought against this (men like Tsunayoshi and Yoshimune) and made efforts to counteract the rising tide of evil by the Kwampo Reforms of 1742, for instance, other Shoguns (like Ieshige and Ieharu) outdid their own vassals in profligacy and love of display.

Hakuin's wrath and contempt against this outrageous life of the upper classes is reflected in his popular sermons. It is depicted in his description of the sinners in states of hell amongst whom are found even purple-robed and red-robed abbots, and many members of very high rank.

Perhaps one of the worst results of the extravagance and luxury of the higher classes was the deepened poverty of the lower masses, amongst whom the chief sufferers were the peasants.

Hakuin's altruism was no doubt the chief incentive for his sympathetic attitude. But this was reinforced by his own personal experiences. The desolation into which Shoin-ji had fallen (the temple at which he became resident priest) almost surpasses description. The property had fallen into the hands of usurers before Hakuin returned at the request of his dying father. The roof was broken and the upright posts holding up the building were rotten. Wind and rain could not be kept out. Only one faithful old servant remained to collect firewood, grow a few vegetables, and do the needful morning and evening chores. Very little rice was collected by the daily alms-collecting bowl, so that it was barely possible to sustain life.

Hakuin, however, found peace, quietness and brightness in this temple just as it was. Here he practised what he called 'introspective meditation', seeking truth within. He said: 'From the day I came here for quiet and restful purity, I became healthier every day. I had no sense of either poverty or wealth. It was as if I were dwelling in an open country of ten thousand leagues.'

This poverty which his bright spirit had thus passed by, was an experience he was able to share with his poor parishioners. He gave them the comfort and help of his own wisdom, as is seen by his wayside sermons and the talks he had with them as he sat by the side of the fields where they were working. They called him 'our dear priest'.

These wayside and field-side talks show that Hakuin could take a good deal of knowledge for granted in his listeners. Besides the traditions which were handed down in their homes, much of the famous scriptures seems to have been understood. Many of them could read, as is shown by his use of ideograms for illustrating his exhortations.

His religious tolerance and skilful use of accommodated truth enabled him to bring the truth home to his listeners' hearts without offending their religious susceptibilities.

The main object of his instruction was to open their eyes to the importance of the mind and the fundamental buddha-nature which is to be found within each of us. He held the prevailing views of the complex nature of the body with its four constituents and two fundamental principles of activity — positive and negative, with the internal organs embodying various mental activities.

This physical foundation being so complicated, it was not surprising that the mind should be even more so. To explain the nature of man to his hearers he used three ideograms, and put his teaching into the form of an allegory drawn from the social life of the time, which would be easily intelligible to them.

The controlling element is explained by the ideogram 'shin' (kami, god). This is likened to the feudal lord who gives unity to all mental and spiritual activities.

Below this lord (shin) come the retainers and close attendants. The ideogram for these is the one generally used for 'sprites', 'gnomes', etc., and for such indefinable qualities as the 'spirit of a flower' or 'an echo'. These retainers stand for the inward qualities of the mind, and point to mental vigour, energy and strength of soul.

In the third place comes the ideogram generally used for such things as air or atmosphere (ki). This stands for the common people, the peasants who till their lord's fields, etc. They represent dispositions, moods and frames of mind.

'*Shin*', then, signifies the unifying aspect of man's mental life. '*Ki*' points to its all-pervasive activity.

This complicated mind is conceived as operating on two levels. The controlling level, the 'mind-king', grasps the phenomenal world in general or perceives objectivity as a whole. It controls the more individual perceptions of objects and may be said to be the realisation of non-self.

The lower level of mind, the 'mind-place', perceives objects separately as individual objects, form and colour. It discriminates and gives rise to differing forms of consciousness, such as memory, desire, imagination. The more inward forms are the retainers. The outward perceptions (of form, etc.) are the peasants. These two levels of mind operate in varied ways. There are, roughly speaking, those which deal with intellectual problems, and those which are concerned with moral matters, and so on.

The important problem about all this complicated organism of the mind, however, is how it came into being, and what is going to be its end. How is it related to the ultimate welfare of mankind? Hakuin tells his readers and listeners to practise what he calls '*naikan*' (introspection) if they wish to answer these questions satisfactorily. This will eventually lead to the knowledge that all sense-consciousness must be brushed away, when enlightenment will result. This will be the deliverance from the terrors of the ever-revolving wheel.

But if all sense-consciousness is brushed aside, is nothing left? Hakuin says that when the 'accumulated dusts' have been brushed off the mirror, true wisdom will come, wisdom which will not cause a return to the wheel. This wonderful wisdom cannot be described. What is it, Hakuin asks, that makes a person into a real artist or musician or craftsman? It is some hidden, mysterious element within, which cannot be told in words.

Hakuin spent the first part of his life in pursuit of this secret, and the second part — when he had found the secret — in helping others along the road to its discovery.

This teaching, Hakuin believed, was to be found by men and women of all ranks of life and even in those forms of Buddhism which differed from his own — the Amida, Shingon, Nichiren and other sects — provided they were sincere and straightforward in their search. But they must not expect to find the way easy. The difficulties of sincere meditation as well as of sincere reverence might be considered as obstacles, but they are obstacles to be overcome, and in the overcoming of them is the assurance of enlightenment for prince and peasant alike.

Hakuin's affectionate interest in his peasant parishioners is shown by his use of their own patois. This cannot, of course, be rendered into a foreign language. Here, however, is a short sentence from the *Anjin hokoritataki*, which shows the kind of language he used in his talks to his humble friends:

Yare, Yare, minasan kiite mo kunnai. Oraga Oyaji wo nan no kuni no ohito mo....

Moreover, in each separate sermon, the language suits the character who is supposed to be speaking. Thus, in the *Otafuku Joro no Kobiki Uta*, we have:

Ten ja, ten ja to minasama osharu. Ten no togame mo iya de soro. Fumi no kazu kazu koi kogaretemo, washi wa toza no hana wa iya!

A Chat on a Boat in the Evening

Yasen Kanna

Preface to A Chat on a Boat in the Evening

A Chat on a Boat in the Evening

The translator wishes to acknowledge the assistance of Father Wilhelm Schiffer S.J. in the translation of parts of the following chapter, an earlier version of which was published in *Monumenta Nipponica*, 1957.

Preface to A Chat on a Boat in the Evening

(Words) Selected by the Starved and Frozen One
of the Hermitage of Poverty.

[A near disciple of Hakuin]

In the spring of the seventh year of the Horeki era (1757),
at the (zodiacal) sign of the Ox in the fourth duodenary
of the calendar, the proprietor of the bookstore, Shogetsu
Do, in the capital, sent a letter written in the current handwriting to the near disciples of our Kokurin (Hakuin). In
this letter he said:

'I have heard with humble respect that there is a manuscript entitled *Yasen Kanna (A Chat on a Boat in the
Evening)* among the papers of your teacher. I am told
that in this work he has put together very carefully the
secrets of long life, secrets which train the spirit,
nourish the soul and supply power for doing work. Indeed, this work contains the essence of what is called
'the divine elixir of life'. Therefore, the wise who
know the good things of the world, think of this book
as they do of a rainbow shining in the clouds after a
long drought. Some wandering monks have transcribed
it, but they keep it hoarded away as a great secret and
do not let it be seen. It is as if the mighty forces of

heaven are kept uselessly stored up in a great chest. My request is that this book may be given a life as long as that of the catalpa tree so that our spiritual thirst may be quenched.

'I hear that your revered teacher, even in his old age, enjoys being helpful to others. So, if you think there is anything which may be of benefit to us ordinary mortals in this writing, surely, surely, he will not grudge it to us.'

This letter, which was sent in duplicate, was presented to the teacher. He smiled. So his disciples opened the box containing the old manuscripts. More than half the papers had been consumed in the bellies of the moths. The disciples, therefore, immediately emended and copied the writings, and now fifty pages have made their appearance. They are being enclosed in proper covers and sent to the capital. I am a day or two older than the other disciples, so I have felt compelled to undertake this preface.

[Hakuin said:] 'This teacher (I myself) has been living in this temple for about forty years. Since I took up my alms bowl, three generations of hempen-robed monks have crossed this threshold. Here they have submitted to my poisonous spittle and endured my painful rod, but they have forgotten to go away. Some have been here for ten or twenty years. Some do not seem to dislike the probability that they may become dust under the trees of this Swan Grove (this temple). They are all of them prominent men, 'fair flowers' for all regions. They live scattered about to the east and west, within ten or twelve miles. They live under conditions of great suffering in old decaying houses, temples and broken-down tombs, which they rent as hermitages. Distressed in the mornings, pained with bitter evenings, starved in the daytime, frozen at night, nothing passes through their mouths but vegetables and barley flour. Their ears hear nothing but scoffs and reviling or scolding words. What touches their bodies is only angry fists and painful rods. What they see causes them to furrow their brows. What they hear brings sweat to their bodies. The very gods must surely shed tears for them. The demons must surely put the palms of their hands together and pray for them.

'When these men first came here, they looked like Sogyoku and Ka-an so attractive were their looks, and their skin shone like fine oil. But before long they were like Koto, their bodies dried up, their faces haggard. If one met them on the Toho shores of the lagoon they were like bent up wizened things. If they were not, in truth, very bodhisattvas, bold and strong of spirit, regarding not the life of their bodies, what pleasure could there possibly have been for them in crowding together here for such a long time? It is because these men have too often suffered excessively and been too strict in their disciplinary exercises that their lungs have shrunk, their bodies have become wizened. They suffer pains in their loins and have indigestion and other diseases which are too hard to cure. For very pity and grief, I myself — never too well and pale — feel that I can no longer restrain myself, but must daily exercise my hoary old head and try to feed them from these aged breasts of mine, by imparting to them the secret of what I call "introspection".[1]

'Let me say here, too, that if anyone who has come to practise meditation and discernment of the Way and is an advanced student, has fits of dizziness and feels weary in his body as if the five internal organs are out of harmony with each other, then even if he tries to cure his ailments by the use of the three medical arts of acupuncture, moxa-cautery and potions, and even if he were Kada or Henso, it would be difficult for him to be healed. But I have the secret of the hermit's elixir of life. My dear friends, I hope you will make trial of it. If you do, you will soon see wonderful results. It will be to you like the sun bursting out in its full brightness through the clouds and mists of night.

'If you wish to practise this secret art, desist for a while from activities, refrain from meditating on the model subjects (koan) and learn to sleep. Before you go to sleep or close your eyes, stretch out your legs and press them tightly together. Let the energy of your whole body fill your body below your navel, breathing centre and loins, and time after time think of the following sort of things: "It is this body of mine — all the parts below my navel and loins — which is nothing other than my own primal, essential dignity. What need then is there of such things as nostrils? This body of mine is my true original home. Why should I need news of my (earthly) home? This body of mine is in very truth the pure paradise of my spirit. What need is there of any further glory? This lowly body of mine is in truth my very own Amida. What dharma can he teach me?"

'Bring such ideas into your mind again and again, and you will find that when the effects of such reflections have taken a hold on you, your body will be stronger, for its energy will fill your loins right down to the soles of your feet, and the lower part of your abdomen will become round like an unused ball. Meditating thus time after time for five or seven days or perhaps up to twenty or thirty-seven days, the five aggregations and six accumulations of sickness, pain and other symptoms of disease, will be cured. If they are not, you may cut off this old monk's head and carry it away with you.

'When my disciples heard this, they were filled with joy and were very grateful. Each one carried on this secret discipline privately and all saw marvellous results. How soon the effects were felt depended on the exactness of their performance. More than half were entirely cured. Each of them continued to praise the wonderful effects of this method of introspection.

'The teacher (I) says, "Do not let this cure of the sickness of your hearts be sufficient. The better the cure, so much the more is the need to carry on the discipline. The better you understand, the more you will progress!" When I first began this method of disciplinary study, I became severely ill. My pains and distress were worse, ten times worse, than you have suffered. It became impossible for me to move, and I used to think in my heart — as people in the world probably think — that I would like to get rid of this old skin bag of bones as quickly as possible rather than go on suffering so much. But, oh, how great my joy was when I was taught the secret of this method of introspection, for I found that I was entirely cured. My joy was like that which all of you feel. A great man once said: "This, indeed, is the divine art of long life and immortality. With this, a life which lasted for three hundred years, would be called only a medium-length life. No one can guess how much longer it may go on."

'My own joy was unlimited. I did not neglect to perform the proper discipline for three years and I noticed that my body was gradually getting better and my vitality was getting stronger. Then I began to think in my inner mind that even though I might be disposed to carry on this discipline and support life for, say, eight hundred years, as did Hoso,

I would be nothing better than a ghost protecting the corpse of dull ignorance. It would be like a badger sleeping in its old burrow. In the end there would be nothing but the dust of destruction. Why have I never yet found such companions as Kakko, Tekkai, Chokwa, and Hicho, those immortal beings? Would it not be better, I thought, to perform the four great vows,[2] to practise the way of the bodhisattvas, to fulfil the works of the dharma, to realise the irreversible firm *dharmakaya* (dharma-body) which is not born and does not die?

'So I secured two or three like-minded colleagues, bodhisattvas, who came to study the mysteries with me. Together with them, I practised the method of introspection, as well as meditation. Together with them, I cultivated the virtues of the ascetic life, and together with them, I struggled for more than thirty years. Each year another two or three members were added to us, until now there are nearly two hundred who have been added to our number. In this fellowship there are monks who have come from all parts of the country, men who have undergone labour, sorrow and weariness. I pitied these men, and privately handed on to them this teaching about introspection, and they were immediately cured. The more they understood, the more did they progress.

'Though my own age is said to have passed that of a withered old tree, I do not suffer from even one pint of painful illness. My teeth have not fallen out, and my eyes and ears are clearer than ever, so that I am apt to forget the darkness and cloudiness of life's end. Never in any month have I had to omit the fortnightly obligations of the dharma. In response to requests from the provinces, I have attended more than fifty or sixty meetings where four or five hundred people have assembled; and I have — in accordance with the wishes of the monks — expressed my views and lectured on the scriptures and records, sometimes for five or seven ten-day periods. Not once have I been obliged to close any meeting before finishing. My body is healthy and my energy is greater now than it was when I was a young fellow of twenty or thirty. All this is entirely due to the method of introspection.

'My disciples who were living with me in the temple, with tears of grateful respectfulness, asked, "Oh, teacher, out of your deep compassion for us, please write down the main points of this method of introspection. Write it so as to preserve it and succour us and those colleagues of ours who, like us, may in future suffer from the weariness which comes from hard meditation." The teacher (I) agreed and immediately this manuscript was written.

'And what is the sum of the teaching of this document? Roughly, it is the teaching that the maintenance of life is better than the moulding of outer forms alone. The essential of the moulding of outer forms consists mainly in pressing the vital forces down to below the navel. When the mind is concentrated in that way and the spirit is intent, then the elixir of life is made. When the elixir is made, then the outer form becomes firm, and when the outer form becomes firm, the inward spirit becomes perfected. When the inward spirit is thus perfected, long life ensues. This is the secret of the nine revolutions of the elixir of hermits (i.e. the most perfect form of the elixir).

'It is of utmost importance and must be well understood that what I mean is that this elixir is not an external thing. It is entirely a descent of the spirit-heart into the space below the navel. If all my resident disciples in this temple are assiduous in performing this discipline and try to progress without carelessness, not only will the meditation sickness be cured and the weariness of the body be overcome, but

A Monk
Meditating

By courtesy of
the Abbot of
Shoin Temple,
Shizuoka-ken.

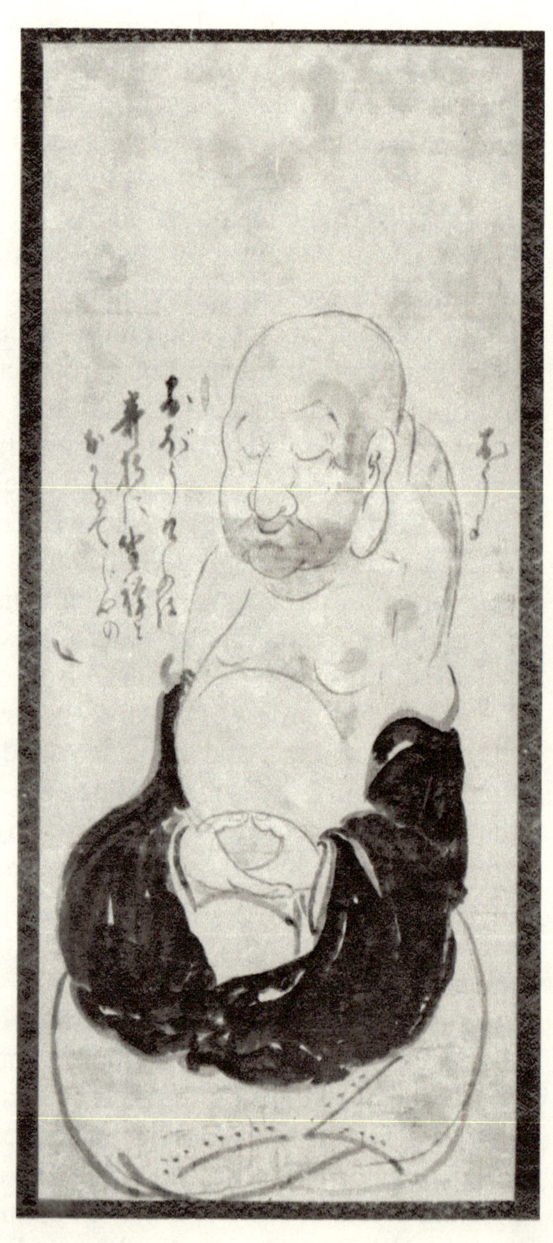

great progress will also be made in Zen itself; and in future years those persons who are now in doubt will be found clapping their hands and laughing for joy.

'But now, look! The moon is high; the shadow of the castle has gone.'

> On the twenty-fifth day, fourth calendar sign, in the spring of the year, in the seventh year of the Horeki era (1757).
> In the temple of distress and poverty, by the hungry and frozen one burning incense and bowing down his head.

A Chat on a Boat in the Evening

Yasen Kanna

On the very first day that I went into the mountains to study and practise meditation, I made up my mind to be strenuous and bold in faith, and to work hard at carrying on the refining discipline of the Way. After only two or three frosts had passed over me, suddenly one night I received an enlightening experience. The many doubts which I had felt up to this time were brought into harmony with the root principles of the inner spirit, and they melted away like ice in water. The karma-roots which produce the life-death cycle, sank to the lowest depths and dissolved like foam on the surface of the sea. I pondered frequently on the quick way in which the karma-cycle eliminated mankind — the twenty or thirty years spoken of by the men of old. Oh, how uncertain they are! Only a few months and they are all forgotten by those who were doing the dancing!

After that night, however, when reflecting on my daily life, those two conditions of life — activity and non-activity — had become entirely out of harmony. The two inclinations in me towards finiteness and infinity had become indistinct in my mind. I could not make up my mind to do or not to do. So the thought occurred to me that I would like to clothe myself in a lustrous glow and throw off my present life and depart from this world.

Finding myself in such a state of mind, I set my teeth, fixed my eyes clearly and determined to forego sleep and food. But before I had spent many months in that strenuous way, my heart began to make me dizzy, my lungs became dry, my limbs felt as cold as if they were immersed in ice and snow, and my ears were filled with ringing like the rushing waters of a swift river in a deep canyon. My inward organs felt weak and my whole body trembled with apprehension and fear. My spirit was distressed and weary, and whether sleeping or waking, I continually saw all sorts of imaginary things, brought to me through my six senses. Both sides of my body were continually bathed in sweat, and my eyes were perpetually filled with tears. I knew that even if I resorted to famous teachers in every part of the country and searched for great physicians in the world, none of the hundred medicines would be of any avail.

It was at this time that someone said to me: 'There is a man living on the cliffs of the mountains of Shirakawa in Yamashiro. People call him Hakuyu and speak of him as 'teacher'. His age, they say, has passed in review three or four full cycles of the years of the Rat (which means that they thought he had lived for about 240 years). His abode is about eight or nine miles from the nearest habitation of people. He does not like seeing anyone and if someone goes up to his dwelling, he runs away so as to avoid them. Some think he is a wise man; others think he is a fool. The villagers speak of him as their own hermit. It is rumoured that he was a teacher of Ishikawa Jozan (1583-1672) of the Takeyama School. He is an expert astronomer and also skilled in medical lore. Not long ago, however, someone did manage to visit him and was fortunate enough to hear some of his rare sayings. This person said that the hermit's words would certainly be of benefit to mankind.'

When I heard this, I said nothing to anybody, clad myself in my travelling garments and started off early one morning whilst the dew was still on the ground. It was the beginning of the first month in the year of the Tiger, in the era of Hoei (1704-1711, i.e. 1710). I crossed over a valley still in deep shadow and hastened to the village of Shirakawa. There I deposited my bundle at a teahouse and made enquiries about the location of Hakuyu's abode. A villager pointed with a stick to a place far up the valley. Guiding myself by the sound of running water I went up this valley for nearly three miles until I reached a place where I had to cross a torrent. Then I struggled through thick underbrush until I came upon an old man who pointed out to me a spot far up in the clouds. There I could just see a gold and silver looking patch, not much bigger than an inch square. As I went on, this little patch was sometimes visible and sometimes lost to view according to the swirling mists of the mountains. I had been told that that was the place where Hakuyu hung a rush curtain at the entrance to his cave-dwelling. I girded up my loins and began the steep climb. After passing some precipitous places, I pushed through more thick underbrush. Ice and snow bit through my straw sandals. The damp mists weighed down my clothes. Sweat poured out of me and my fat flowed away. At last I reached the little rush curtain.

Here I stopped for a moment and looked at the scenery. The surroundings were of an infinite purity and everything seemed sublime. The universe of phenomena was truly up-lifting. My spirit trembled and I was filled with awe. For a short time, I leant against a rock and inhaled the sweet air. Then I shook out my garments, straightened out my collar and hesitatingly and deferentially peered through the little rush curtain. There I could dimly see Hakuyu sitting upright with his eyes fixed straight in front of him. His luxuriant hair reached his knees. His face was ruddy and as beautiful as the fruit of the jujube tree. He was wearing a large cloth as an apron and was seated on a soft straw mat.

The cave itself was barely six feet square. There was absolutely no furniture nor anything necessary for living purposes, and no food, only a small desk on which were placed three books: The *Mean of Confucius,* the *Tao Te Ching* by Lao Tzu, and the *Diamond Wisdom Sutra* (the *Vajracchedika Prajnaparamita Sutra).*

I made a courteous bow of respect and told the old hermit carefully what the symptoms were of my illness and asked for his advice and help. He opened his eyes and fixed them on me, and very slowly he said: 'I am a man living here in these mountains, more dead than alive. I sleep in the company of deer. I gather chestnuts for my food. How can I have knowledge of anything else? I am really quite ashamed that I should have been the cause of troubling a self-sacrificing monk like you to come and visit me.'

On hearing these words, I became more urgent and continued with my request 'knocking at his door', so to speak. Then Hakuyu quietly took my hand and began to enquire about my five internal organs (heart, liver, stomach, lungs and kidneys) and went on to investigate the nine marks (colour, fingernails etc.). My fingernails were only half an inch long (half what they should have been). He furrowed his brow as if he were in pain, and said: 'Alas! Your meditation has been too unmeasured and your asceticism too strict. The chance of a cure has been lost. You are too seriously ill. This meditation sickness of yours will indeed be difficult to cure. Even if you were to try all the three curative measures (acupuncture, moxacautery and potions) hoping to be cured by them, and even if the most famous doctors were to use all their medical knowledge, you would not see any wonderful results. You are already defeated because of your excessive meditation practices. Unless you now heap up the goodness of the method of introspection you will find that at last you will not even be able to stand.' And by 'stand' he meant literally standing on my feet.

So I said: 'Please, I would like to hear the essential secrets of this method of introspection. Whilst studying it, I will practise it as carefully as I can.'

Hakuyu remained silent as he slowly changed his posture. Then very quietly he said: 'Ah, sir, you are the sort of person who likes to ask many questions. Shall I tell you a little of what I learnt long ago? I learnt the mysterious key to the knowledge of preserving life. It is something which but few people know. Providing one is not remiss in carrying out this system, wonderful results will certainly be obtained. A long life may be expected. For, you see, the Great Way is divided into two fundamental principles — the negative and positive, the yin and yang. When these two are in harmony, people of character are produced, for then there is an innate vitality silently moving within the body. The five organs are so arranged that the rhythmical movements of the pulse act correctly. The breathing which protects the body, and the blood which gives it activity, mutually rise and fall in regular motion about fifty times each day and night. To each full exhalation there is a rhythmic movement of about three inches, and so too for each full inhalation. There are about 13,500 full breathings in and out during a full day and night.

'The heart is doing its work regularly and easily. The lungs do not get tired or become heated with their constant effort to keep in tune with an excited heart. None of the elements which make up the material of the body are worked to exhaustion, nor are the five activities of life (obtaining nourishment, movement, perceptiveness, study and realisation of the purpose of life); these are all carried on with ease. Nor do the six "dependants", by which I mean the six sense organs, become fixed, and therefore the chief fundamentals of the bodily structure remain unimpaired.

'But when these two fundamental principles are out of harmony, the structure of the body goes awry; each part and all the elements of it become disordered, and any or all of the hundred diseases may result. In that case none of the hundred medicines will provide any remedy. All the physicians in the world, joining hands in consultation, will not be able to do or even say anything useful.

'But let me put it another way. The maintenance of the life of our bodies may be compared to the defending of a country. Enlightened princes and sages always give their attention to the masses. Unenlightened rulers, on the other hand, only pay attention to the upper classes. Now, when this happens the "nine lords" assert their own authority and the "hundred lesser lords" call for special consideration for themselves, so that in the final event there is nobody to take care of the poverty and distress of the common folk. At such times, though the country may look green, there will be nothing but starvation and death amongst ordinary people. Virtue is hidden away, the people will be angry and discontented, local nobles will isolate themselves or rebel, and the barbarians who surround the land, will rival one another with their raids and uprisings, until at last the common people will be reduced to the direst distress, and the rhythmic order of the national life will come to an end.

'But when attention is devoted to the masses, the "nine lords" restrain their ambitions, the "hundred lesser lords" observe their agreements sincerely and do not forget the hard labour of the poor and common people. In the fields there is enough millet and some to spare. There is enough and more than enough material for clothing. The wise men of the provinces join up with the nation, the local nobles are submissive and afraid to offend, and the common people are well nourished. The whole nation is strong. No one dares to oppose the laws, and no enemies make incursions on the land. The land does not hear the sound of war drums, and the people do not even know the meaning of the word "halberd".

'And it is just like that with the human body. The person of character always looks after the needs of the body in a reasonable way. When the organs are reasonably cared for, the "seven evils" do not function in the body, nor do the "four heresies" invade it from outside. The bodily defences are so strong that the heart and mind are healthy. The mouth does not have to taste the bitterness of potions, nor does any part of the body have to experience the pains of acupuncture or moxacautery.

'But the one who follows the current of folly, selfishly turns his attention to what he calls "high estates". This causes a disorganisation of all the material elements of the body. So the "five officials" (i.e. the main internal organs), shrink from fatigue, and the "six relatives" (i.e. the organs of sense) suffer and become inharmonious. This is why an official (at Shitsu-en, Chi-yuan) said, "The true man in breathing, breathes through his heels; the common man in breathing breathes through his throat." Kyo-shun said,

"When the spirit is in the lower (parts), the breathing is from afar (scarce), when it is in the upper (parts), the breathing becomes short." Jo-yo shi said, "In man there is the spirit of real unity. When that descends below the navel, the "positive" returns. If one wants to know the time when that "positive" returns, the sign is the heat (of the body). Roughly speaking, for maintaining life, the upper parts of the body should be kept pure and cool, and the lower parts warm. Then the twelve pulses and the twelve branches (veins) will be in agreement and in accord with the twelve months and the twelve hours (of the day). This is just the same as when the six lines of the system of divination *(I Ching)* complete the circuit and the year is completed. When the five negative lines are on top and one positive line is at the bottom (of the divination sign), this represents the winter solstice. This is what is meant, perhaps, by breathing through the heels. When the three positive lines are on top and the three negative lines are at the bottom (of the divination sign), this points to the beginning of spring, when all things are full of the spirit of growth and the hundred herbs receive the abundance of the growth of springtime. When the perfect man energetically fills the lower parts, this is the sign that when he has received this energy, his powers of resistance are complete and his spiritual power is great.

'When the five negative lines of divination are underneath (in the divination sign) and one positive line is on top, this means deprivation. It is the season of the ninth month. When the sky receives this, the trees and gardens lose their colours, the hundred herbs wither away. This is the sign that the ordinary man in breathing is breathing through his throat, and his looks become emaciated, and his teeth fall out. And that is why in the *Enjusho (Yen-*

shouju) it says: "When the six positive lines give out, all the lines are negative and men easily die."

'So one ought to know for certain that one should energetically fill the lower part of the body with spiritual energy, and this is essential for nourishing life.

'In ancient times, Go Kai-sho went to see the teacher, Seki-dai, and after performing the ablutions he asked about the art of making the elixir. The teacher said: 'With me is the mysterious secret of the original and true elixir, and unless it is to the very highest "vessels" (i.e. persons), it must not be handed on. In old times Kwo-se-shi told this to the Emperor Kwo (Huang, the Yellow Emperor, legendary date approximately four thousand years ago). After the Emperor had performed the thirty-seven ablutions,[3] he accepted it. For outside the Great Way, there is no true elixir, and outside the true elixir, there is no Great Way. After all, there is the dharma of the five (methods of) getting rid of desires (coming from the five senses). When you have got rid of your desires, and your five senses have forgotten their functions, then the primary and true spirit will similarly fill your whole vision. This is what that Great White Hermit (or man of the Way) said: "I who serve heaven am united with the heaven which I serve." This is the overflowing spirit spoken of by Mencius. This is to be stored below the navel, preserved for years and months. This is to be made unconquerable. And then one morning one lights the fire in the oven of the elixir, the external and the internal and all in between — the eight fastenings and the six bindings — will all together become the one great elixir. Then one will for the first time understand that one's self was born before the heavens and the earth, and that it will not die after the great void, and that it is the true and eternal divine "hermit". This is the time when the true elixir oven is successful. How could such a one have pleasure in such magic doings as driving the winds, striding on the mists, pushing down the land, walking on water and such "closed-up" things? He may stir up the ocean into cream, or turn the soil into gold, but as has been said by the ancients: "The elixir is below the navel, the fluid is the fluid of the lungs. One turns down the fluid of the lungs to the space below the navel and turns the lung fluid into the elixir."'

Here I said, 'I have listened to your words with respect, and I will cease from my Zen meditation for a time and take the opportunity of trying to tranquillise myself. What I am afraid of is what Rishisai called "a tendency to diarrhoea", and if I keep my mind on one place, won't my spirit and blood become stagnant?'

Hakuyu said with a smile, 'No, no. That teacher, Ri, said that fire rises, so make it come down. It is the nature of water to come down, so make it rise. Water rising, fire descending — this is called 'mixing'. When these things mix together they are perfected; when they do not mix they are still imperfect. Mixing is the sign of life; non-mixing is the sign of death. When that teacher, Ri, spoke of the tendency to diarrhoea as a purifying symptom, he was trying to help those who study at the Tankei School of Medicine. These people used to say that the premier fire ascends easily and the whole body suffers, and those suffering parts supply water in order to control that fire. There are two principles in the premier of fire. The 'lord' fire is above and rules in quietness; the 'premier' fire has its place underneath and controls movement. The lord fire controls the heart; the premier assists it. The premier fire is of two sorts: one becomes the kidneys and one the liver. The liver is like thunder; the kidneys are like the dragon. And that is why it has been said that when the dragon is made to descend into the depths of the sea, there is no loud thunder, but when the thunder is hidden in a marsh, most certainly no dragon will fly out. Whether sea or marsh, both imply water. Is not this then a word showing that fire, which rises so easily, must be kept under control? Again it is said: "When the heart is weary, it will be emptied and warm. When the heart is empty, in order to assist it, the heart is brought down and mixed with the kidneys." This is called restoring it. It is the way of completed perfection.

'Sir, your fire heart has been going the wrong way, upwards, hence your chronic sickness. Unless you bring it down again, even though you exhaust all the secrets of the three worlds, you will not be able to stand.

'Is my plan — which is so like that of the Way *(tao)* — to be considered very different from that of Shakyamuni's? It is Zen. When suddenly it starts working, you will find yourself laughing. For, surely, meditation through non-meditation becomes true meditation. Too much meditation must be said to be heretical meditation. Sir, facing your previous over-meditation, you are now seeing these severe sicknesses. Now, in order to save yourself from these sicknesses, it must be by non-meditation. Do you not think so? Sir, gather together the flames of fire of your heart and place them under your navel and below your feet. Then your whole chest will become cool, and you will not have a single worrying thought; no single drop of a wave of desire will disturb the waves of consciousness. This is the true and pure meditation.

'And do not say that you will leave off Zen meditation for a while. Buddha said that a hundred and one diseases are cured by putting your heart in your feet. Moreover, there is in the *Agamas* a rule about how to use cream, which is a wonderful thing for saving a person from the weariness of heart. Then in the *Mahashikwan* (Chi-k'ai's *Scripture on Meditation*, 538-597) of the Tendai teaching, the causes of disease are exhaustively examined, and detailed disquisitions are given as to rules about curing sicknesses. There are twelve kinds of breathings which help in curing all diseases. There is also the rule about seeing a bean, as it were, below the navel. The purpose of doing this is to bring down the fire of the heart and concentrate it below the navel and right down to the soles of the feet. This not only cures diseases, but helps greatly in Zen meditation. In the last analysis there are two kinds of 'stopping' and 'meditation' (*shamatha* and *vipashyana*), the relative and the absolute. The absolute one is the complete vision of the absolute reality. The relative one prioritises fixing the mind on the protecting fire of the heart by concentrating pressure below the navel. Ascetics who have used this method have received much benefit from it.

'In ancient times the patriarch of Eihei-ji (i.e. Dogen, or Shoyo Daishi, founder of the Soto sect, 1200-1253), went to the China of the Sung Dynasty and paid a visit to Nyojo at the Tendo monastery. One day he entered the "Hall of Mysteries" and asked what might help him in his meditations. Nyojo said: "Dogen, at the time of meditation, fix your attention on the palm of your left hand." This is the summary of what Gishi (Chih-kai) taught about stopping and meditation. Gishi was the first to teach the secret of this stopping and meditation in connection with introspection. By this method he saved one of his disciples, Chinshin, from serious illness and snatched him from a thousand deaths.[4] Again, the monk Haku-un (1043-1121), said: "I always make my heart fill my abdomen. I never fail to do this when, for instance, I am instructing my disciples, presiding at meetings, associating with guests, at special meetings, holding services, or at the seven verticals, where salvation by one's own efforts is taught, or at the eight horizontals, where salvation by the help of Amida is taught.[5] I know, too, that many aged guests of mine have benefited. It is a practice much to be valued."

'Here, in summary is what appears in the *So-mon (Su wen)*: If one is quiet and empty, the true spirit follows on. If the pure spirit is protected within, from where can illnesses come? Am I not pleased to base my word on this? And so it is essential to protect this inside one, and to fill the whole body with fundamental energy as well as to keep the 360 joints and all the 84,000 pores of the skin in perfect state, so that not one of them falls out. It should be known that this is of extreme importance in nourishing life.

'Hoso said: "Here is the rule for keeping the spirit peaceful and directing the vital energy into the correct channels: First, close the doors of the meditation chamber and lie quietly on the floor. Have your pillow two and a half inches high. Stretch out your body and lie face up. Then, close your eyes and concentrate your mind on your chest and diaphragm. Place a goose feather on your nose and do not move until you have inhaled three hundred times. Now, listen to nothing and look at nothing. When you have reached the state where you neither hear nor see anything, neither cold nor heat can violate you, and no bee or scorpion can poison you. Your life will last for 360 years (six of the sexagenary cycles), and you will be near to being a true person.

'Again, Ho of the College of Literature (in China) said: "If you are hungry, take food, but leave off before repletion. Then ramble about for long distances and make your stomach empty. After that, enter a quiet room, sit down in the correct posture, and be silent. Count your inhalations and exhalations, beginning from one to ten, then on from ten to a hundred, and from a hundred continue to one thousand. You will then find that your body will be as still and your spirit as calm as the void itself. When this state has been reached and has lasted for some time, your breath will automatically stop. When your breathing in and out has stopped, your breath will come out like a steaming cloud of vapour from all the 84,000 pores of your body. At this point, all illnesses, permanent and chronic, will automatically be eliminated, and you will understand clearly that all your troubles and handicaps have been destroyed in a most natural way. It will be as if a blind man had suddenly received his sight. He will no longer have to ask someone to point out the way. All that you have to do then, is to give up worldly speech and sustain your vital energy. For it is said: "He who nurtures the eye-sense, always keeps his eyes shut; he who nourishes the ear-sense is always sated (by noises); he who nourishes the heart is always silent."'

Here I interrupted him and said, 'I want to ask you to tell me the rules about how to make use of that cream.' Hakuyu replied, 'If the one who meditates has the four elements out of harmony and feels his body and spirit to be wearied with labour, he must rouse himself and let the following ideas come into his mind. First he has the idea of placing a deliciously scented, pure and clean cream as large as a duck's egg on his head. He will then feel a marvellous sensation come over his whole body. His head will become moist. That moist feeling will seem to sink deeper and go lower and lower to the shoulders, elbows, breasts, diaphragm, lungs, liver and stomach, until at last it reaches the bottom of the spine and the buttocks. Then, the "five gatherings" and "six accumulations" within the breast, and the pains in the bowels, will flow downwards like water until what is left is a sensation of energy circulating round the whole body, warming both legs and reaching right down to the soles of the feet.

'Anyone practising meditation should try to have this sensation more than once. The overflow of energy which goes on sinking in and accumulates until it brims over, warming and moistening the body, is similar to when a good physician collects all kinds of herbs and scented potions, brews them and pours them into a bath until they brim over, and then applies them and makes them soak into every part of a patient's body below the navel.

'When this impression has occurred (because it is a spiritual phenomenon), the senses are intensified. The sense of smell becomes aware of rare odours, and the sense of touch becomes marvellously keen. The body and spirit are so closely in harmony that there is more vitality than when it is only twenty or thirty years old. Now all the "accumulations and gatherings" in the breast melt away; the bowels and stomach become quiet; and imperceptibly the skin takes on a shining glow. Provided one does not then become remiss, there is not a single malady that cannot be cured. What virtue may not then be attained? What ascetic practice may not then be performed? What Way may not then be accomplished?

'The rate at which these wonders become efficacious depends solely on the perfection — "the purity or coarseness" — of the person who is practising the art. When I was very young, I suffered from many illnesses, ten times more serious than those from which you are suffering. I reached such a state of disease that no physician would consider my case, and in spite of making exhaustive use of the hundred remedies, there was no medical art which could save me. Thereupon, I prayed to the gods, and I asked for help from many deities. Oh, how fortunate I was at last, when I received from someone the knowledge of this wonderful "cream treatment"! My joy was limitless, and without intermission, I practised this discipline until in almost no time half my illnesses had left me. From that time on, both outwardly in my body and inwardly in my spirit, I have known nothing but calm and peace.

'Gradually, but with assiduous practise, hardly noticing the waxing and waning of the moon or marking the passing of the years, my worldly thoughts became less and less, and lighter; and now it is as if I have forgotten the old habits of my human desires. I do not even know how many tens of years have passed over me, but somewhere in the middle of my life, I had occasion to go into the mountains of Wakayama Prefecture, where I escaped from the world for about thirty years. During all that time, I had no communication with mankind. When I look back on that period, it seems like a short dream; a dream of millet, yellow, but only half ripened.

'Now, up here in this uninhabited mountain, I have cast away this withered old vessel of my body. I clothe it with only two or three thin cloths even in the most severe winter nights when the cold would normally break through the thickest woollen garments, yet I have never suffered any harm from cold in these worn out old insides of mine. It is now many months since my supply of stored grain gave out and I have received no other grain, yet I have never felt frozen or starved. I am sure that all this is due to the wonderful impressions (made on me by the knowledge of this method of meditation). What I have told you is a mysterious matter which cannot be rationally discovered throughout a long life. And now, what more is there for me to say?'

With these words he closed his eyes and remained sitting in silence. With tears in my eyes I expressed my thanks to him and slowly left the cave. The rays of the setting sun were just tinting the tops of the trees below and I started to make my way down the valley. After a short time, however, I heard the sound of footsteps echoing behind me. I timidly turned and looked back. With surprise and wonder, I saw that Hakuyu had left his cave and was coming to show me the way. He said: 'This mountain trail shows but uncertain traces of the footsteps of man. It is difficult to distinguish east from west here. I was afraid that you, who have been a guest of mine, should be distressed on your way home.' The old fellow said he would show me the way. He was wearing straw sandals such as are generally shod on young horses, and he carried a thin stick, but he stepped over the rough rocks and climbed up the precipitous places like the wind waving over a level plane. Laughing and chatting, he went in front of me as my guide. When we had descended the track for about two miles, we reached the river which I was to ford. Here he said: 'If you follow down this river you will certainly reach the village of Shirakawa.'

I reluctantly parted from him, but for some time stood and followed him with my eyes as he retraced his steps. The pace of his old feet was strong and swift, like that of a man who was flying to a mountain retreat to escape the world. I envied him and respected him, and felt bitter with myself because I could not follow a man like that to the very end of the world. Then I slowly turned away.

After that I practised introspection continuously, and before only three years had passed — even though I had not taken any medicines or received any treatments by acupuncture or moxacautery — all those former illnesses of mine had been thoroughly swept away as if by some pre-determined fate. And not only were my illnesses healed, but also those things which were difficult to understand, those things which were difficult to enter into or penetrate, and which until then I had been unable to grasp with my hands or feet, or get my teeth into. I now penetrated them intuitively, right to their roots and down to their depths. And I have experienced this joy six or seven times. Besides all this, I have forgotten just how many times I have experienced 'little visions' — those joys which make one dance. For the first time, I realised the meaning of the words: 'The eighteen great enlightenments of wonderful joy, and the little joys which are without number.' In truth, I have not been deceived.

Previously, even though I had put on two or three pairs of socks, the soles of my feet were as cold as if frozen in snow or ice. Now, though three extremely cold winters have passed over me, I have not worn socks at all, nor have I gone near a fire; and though my years have passed beyond the usual span, there is not half a pint of sickness in me to which I can point. I put all this down to the instruction given me in this heavenly art.

So do not say of me: 'Kokurin, who has one foot in the grave, has written meaningless and absurd nonsense and is trying to deceive people of good class.'

This tradition, of which I have written, is one which has bones as well as spirit. It has not been prepared for those fine people who want to be perfect in an instant.

Those who are sick and tired, and fools like me, will certainly be relieved to some extent if they look, read, and meditate carefully and with detailed study. What I am afraid of is that some people might clap their hands and laugh, and that is why 'the horse munches the dried chaff and disturbs the midday siesta'.

> Dated in the Horeki era (1757), the year of the Ox of the Hi-no-to sign, on the twenty-fifth day, the day called Hei,[6] (Shepherd's Purse) (14th March 1757).

The Embossed Tea Kettle

Orate Gama[7]

Reply to a Near Retainer of Lord Nabeshima of Sesshu Province

Letter Written to a Sick Monk Living in a Distant Province

Reply to an Aged Nun of the Hokke Sect

Hakuin's
Handwriting

By courtesy of
the Abbot of
Shoin Temple,
Shizuoka-ken.

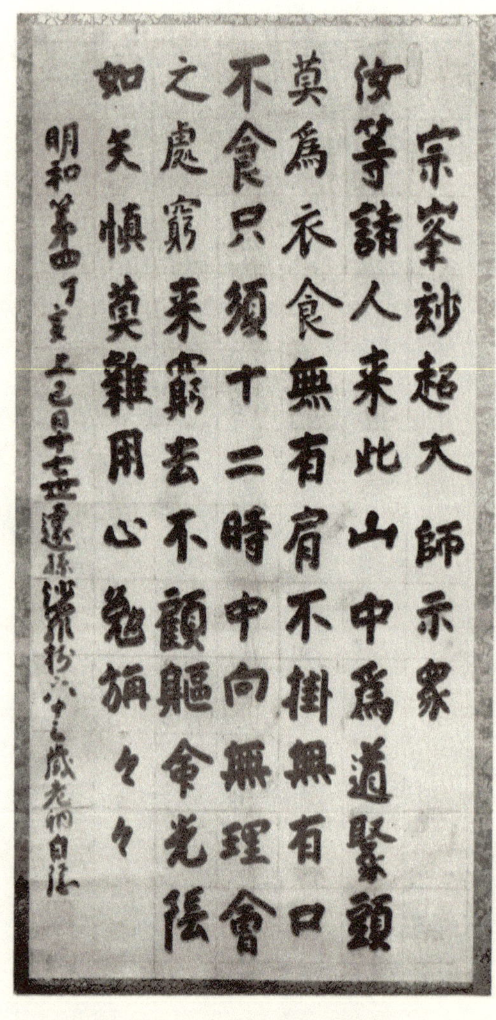

Reply to a Near Retainer of Lord Nabeshima of Sesshu Province

Y ou must, I am sure, feel a great relief now that your long journey of inspection of the harvest crops is safely concluded and your Korean feast satisfactorily finished. My old bodily tabernacle is safe, but I do not intend to trouble you about myself.

I am much interested in your ceaseless exertions in carrying on your plans of the 'two stages of activity and quiet meditation'. What you say is unusual and of great weight. With regard to the other matters mentioned in your letter, each and every one of them accords well with my own sentiments. They are extremely commendable and I, an old monk, rejoice greatly.

As a general rule, if the mental attitude of those who undertake austerities and spiritual discipline is not correct during their times of deliberately planned concentration, they will find themselves hindered in both states of meditation: the state known as 'activity' and that known as 'quiet' or 'calm'. When the mental attitude is wrong, a barrier will be set up between these two states, a barrier of two extremes. One extreme is that of 'darkness' and the other is that of 'scattering'.[8] Moreover, bodily ailments will occur, such as dizziness or a painful shrinking of the lungs;

and physical vitality will be lost, so that illnesses difficult to heal will occur frequently. On the other hand, if the training is carried out properly and in accordance with the true method called 'introspection', the discipline will be thoroughly compatible with the secrets of the preservation of health. Both the body and the mind will be strong and firm, physical vitality will be great, and the carrying out of the dharma will in every way be easy and pleasant.

Now, in the *Agama* sutras minute instructions are given concerning the correct method of regulating one's self for the purpose of coming to the 'great enlightenment'. Also, Chisha (538-597) founder of the Tendai School in China, gave a very thorough explanation of the main idea of this discipline in his book, the *Mahashikwan,* or *Scripture of Samadhi.* A fundamental theme of his book is that, whatever teaching one is studying, whatever dharma one desires to contemplate, and whether one sits upright or not, or carries on the services of sacred processions[9] for six hours or not — whatever one is doing — one should concentrate one's attention, say, on the navel or loins. This concentration of one's attention must never be relaxed, even when the pressure of worldly business is excessive, or when one is entertaining guests. Whatever, do not forget to concentrate the mind on the body.

It not infrequently happens that when people take care of their health in the way mentioned here, they will be able to sit in meditation for a whole day without becoming dulled or wearied, and even if they were to recite the sutras day and night, they would not become tired. Or if they were to write all day long, they would feel no distress. And again, if they were to give instruction in the dharma the whole day, they would not break down. No matter how many works of merit such people were to perform, there would be no onset of sluggishness, but rather their tired, heavy minds would become freer and more generous, and their mental vitality would become greater and greater. On the most painfully hot day, people like that would not feel the need to use a fan, nor even would they perspire. And on the coldest snowy night of a severe winter, they would not have to wear thick clothes, nor would they want to go near a fire to warm themselves. And yet again, even if they were to live to be over a hundred years old, their teeth would remain firm, so that if they remained careful and not negligent, they would reach a great age.

When the conditions mentioned above are properly carried out, there is no Way which cannot be performed. What rule is there that could not be observed? What *dhyana* or mystic meditation is there that could not be practised? What virtue is there, that could not be brought to perfection?

If, however, the ancient practice as mentioned above, is not performed, and the secret of the true discipline is not correctly memorised, and if one seeks to explain the teachings and to understand things in one's own arbitrary way, then the stage of reasonable contemplation will pass, and the opportune time for thought will be lost. As a result, one's throat and chest will become stopped up, one's legs will be as cold as ice, one's ears will ring with noises like echoes in a deep valley, one's lungs will become painfully constricted, and the fluids of one's body will dry up, until at last a disease difficult to heal will come upon one, and life itself will be endangered. And all this would be because the correct method of the true discipline is not known, which would be a truly pitiable state of affairs.

Now, in the book to which I have referred (the *Mahashikwan Sutra* of Chisha) we find mention of what are called the 'relative samadhi' and the 'absolute samadhi'. What I am now writing to you about is a sort of summary of this teaching of the 'relative samadhi' in its connection with the method or dharma of introspection.

When I was young, I had quite the wrong idea about this matter. I used to think that the Way of the Buddha was nothing other than keeping the mind in absolute calm and quiet. I was always searching out dismal places and sitting there as if I was dead. My chest was choked up, as it were, with what were only trivial matters of worldly business. My mind was distracted. And I was unable to enter into any active way of life. So, alarming distresses crowded round me. My mind and body were perpetually in a state of weakness. I was constantly sweating under my arms, and my eyes were continually filled with tears. My mind, too, was all the time bothered with grievances. I had not the least impression that I had obtained any power by means of the Way.

And then I was extremely fortunate. I received guidance concerning the secret method of 'introspection'. I practised this method by myself for three years. The illness, which had until that time been practically incurable, now began to melt away like frost in the morning sunlight. Poisonously hard meditation problems, difficulties of faith, difficulties preventing me from penetrating through to the truth, difficulties in expounding and explaining the teaching, and difficulties which hindered the beginning of periods of meditation — all these things which I had not been able to get my teeth into — all of them without exception, were softened and alleviated, together with my bodily sickness; and they melted away like ice.

And now, this year, having passed the average length of a man's life, I have ten times as much vitality as I had when I was thirty or forty years of age. My body and spirits are healthy and strong. I no longer sweat under my arms; and though I have sometimes refrained from lying down or reclining for two, three or even seven days at a time, my mental energy has not deteriorated. Surrounded by three hundred or five hundred earnest monks, I have taught from the sutras and expounded the mystic records for periods of thirty or fifty days at a time without feeling exhausted. I realise that this is due to the effects of practising 'introspection'.

At first, my main object in carrying out this method was simply for health preservation, but in the course of continuing, and though I did not consciously search for it, I discovered that my power of understanding was awakened. How often I experienced this, I cannot recall.

The most important thing to remember is to carry on the correct discipline by oneself within one's own heart, and not to pick and choose for one's own selfish desires either one or other of the two conditions of life, that is to say, the life of activity or the life of calm. Sometimes, one is tempted to think that the life of calm helps one to progress, whilst the life of activity does not seem to help at all. But those who try to carry on solely with the life of calm, will sooner or later find that they are unable to enter into active life at all. If those people who continuously lead the life of calm, at some time or other have to enter active life with its worldly affairs, they may find that they entirely lose all the advantages they thought they had attained in their quiet place of meditation. Such people will find that they have lost every jot of spiritual vitality which they thought they had gained, and will probably find they are inferior even to the people of the world who have not given any attention to spiritual matters. They might also find that all sorts of rubbishy ideas revolve in their minds, as well as feelings of fear which they did not expect any more. Even quite small jobs will frequently seem to be of enormous weight. They will then discover that they have nothing to show for all their pains in living the life of calm.

For reasons such as these, Daie Zenshi (1089-1163) wrote that the method of the life of activity is a million times better than the method of calm. Another sage, Hakusan, also said that unless the life of activity is fully lived, one may be like a man carrying a great weight of one hundred pounds and climbing up to the top of Mount Yo-gaku.

But you must not think that all I have said means you should dislike or cease trying to continue with the discipline of the life of calm, and deliberately seek to live only the life of activity. The less one understands and knows about these two conditions of life — the active and the calm — the more careful should one be to value them both and remember that they are merely two aspects of one uniform condition. This is what is meant when it is said that one who is really practising meditation does not know that he is walking when he is walking, or sitting when he is sitting. When one has come to a realisation of the nature of the reality of self,[10] then there is nothing which excels the life of activity as a means of attaining that vital power which can be used in any and every place.

Say, for example, a rich man entrusted a hundred pieces of gold to a servant and told him to guard it; and that servant shut himself up in his room, bolted the doors, and sat guarding the treasure so that no one could rob him. Now, such a man's work can by no means be said to be lacking in energy. However, one might compare such a man with a disciple who practises a one-sided discipline of calm for himself alone (*shravaka*).

If, on the other hand, a servant is told to carry the gold to some other place which would entail passing through territories where robbers might surround him like wasps, and thieves might troop round him like ants, then that man would have to be bold and brave, gird a sword, step high, and carry his treasure on a pole, in order to get it safely to its destination without any confusion or mistake. Such a man would show no sign of fear. He would work hard, and everybody would praise his valour and strength. In this case, the man might be compared to a bodhisattva of the 'quick' and 'perfect' Way who seeks nirvana, not only for his own sake, but also for the purpose of teaching all sentient beings.

The treasure of hundreds of pieces of gold represents the determination or will to carry out meditation firmly, irreversibly, with concentrated, deep mindfulness. The robbers who surround him like wasps and the thieves who troop around him like ants, represent the delusions, the bonds binding one to the wheel of existence, the lusts, and false views. The man in the second part of the story represents the bodhisattva who performs the correct meditative discipline perfectly in the 'quick' way, and has thoroughly investigated the truth. The 'place' to which he takes the treasure represents the 'treasure place' of the great calm of the other shore where there are 'four virtues' of perpetual happiness and purity. This is why it is said that the one who comes to meditate truly and correctly, must sit facing the innermost sanctuary of truth.

With regard to the *'shravakas'* ('listeners' of the dharma, or disciples of the 'lower grade'), they are sometimes too lightly thought of. People of our present time often cannot match them, either in their seeking of the Way, or in the brightness of their knowledge and virtue. People today all too often carry on their discipline with poor motives. They are fond only of places where the talk is nothing but tittle-tattle. They do not know the correct behaviour of the bodhisattvas, nor do they have the proper 'cause and effect' relationship with the Buddha Land. The Tathagata criticised and even scolded such people by comparing them to the leprous, itching body of a field fox; and likened them to the nature of scorched reeds and rotten seed.

The third patriarch, Seng-ts'an (Sosan, d. 606), said: 'If your desire is to attain to knowledge of the endlessness of the chain of causation, which is the teaching of the "One Vehicle", you do not have to hate the "six dusts" which darken the mind.' Of course, by these words he did not mean that we may be fond of the 'six dusts'. What the patriarch meant is that just as a waterbird does not get its wings wet when it goes into the water, so we must simply continue to practise our correct method of meditative discipline, being careful neither to reject nor to cling to these 'six dusts'. If you absolutely avoid the 'six dusts' and are fearful of the 'eight winds' which disturb the mind (i.e. profit and loss, praise and blame, fame and disrepute, pleasure and pain), then you will be broken, you will be ground to pieces in the mortar of the lower levels of discipleship, and you will never realise perfect buddhahood.

Another ancient sage, Yoka Daishi, a disciple of Hui-neng (665-713) in the same connection said: 'The practice of true meditation must still be within the sphere where desires exist. It works from within that sphere in order to interpret the meaning of the facts of existence. From within the fire, the lotus blossoms, but even to the very end it never gets soiled with mud.' Now this saying, again, does not mean that one might be addicted to the 'five lusts'. What it really means is that, even if one is surrounded by the 'five lusts' and 'six dusts', all these lusts and dusts are to be treated with the same purity of mind and simplicity of life, just like the lotus which is not soiled by mud. Even if someone goes to live in a forest or on a mountain far away in the countryside, and eats only one egg a day, or fasts entirely, and practises the discipline of meditation for six hours each day, that person can never be absolutely free (from these dusts and lusts) in practising the Way. Much less then, when a man is living in the close fellowship of life with brothers and sisters or with a wife, and with all the confused 'dust-raising' affairs of village life. In all these cases, unless one has the eyes to discriminate the true nature of things, one will not be able to meet the demands of the true discipline, even to an infinitesimal degree, which is why Bodhidharma said: 'If you desire to seek Buddha, you must be able to discriminate concerning the true nature of things.'

But now, if suddenly one's understanding is opened to realise that all aspects of reality are but one, and that there is in truth only one buddha-way, then even the 'six dusts' will be part of the meditation and the 'five lusts' will also be part of that same meditation — for all of one's acts, all of one's words, all of one's activities and all of one's quiet times are included in the true method and practice of meditation. If such is indeed the case, then that form of meditative life in forests and mountains is as far from being the only way to true attainment, as heaven is from earth. Bodhidharma was neither blaming nor praising the ascetic, one who is rather uncommon in the world, when he compared a seeker's life to the lotus living in the midst of fire.

The sage, Yoka Daishi, attained to the inner mystery of the Tendai teaching, which is that the three realities[11] — the absolute, the phenomenal, and the assumed — are in fact but one. He had practised the discipline of *samadhi* with meticulous care, and in the record of his own life he tells us that, according to the way one looks at the matter, there is good and there is bad in whichever of the four postures (walking, sitting, standing and reclining) one takes up for meditation. At the foundation of all, there can be real contemplative *samadhi*. What he says is of course only 'half a word and one ideogram' (teaching suited to beginners), but in any case, it is extremely difficult to carry out the teaching that one can meditate in any of the four postures. When he tells us that *samadhi* is actually concealed within or preserved under these four postures, i.e. that it can be carried on in whatever posture one is in, he is trying to tell us that the whole system of sense-knowledge is contained in those four postures. They are in themselves a form of *samadhi*, and *samadhi* is in truth one with them. His 'bodhisattva' is one who, without rising from his seat or without leaving his monastery, manifests enlightenment through any of the four postures. The four postures are also attitudes of mind, of mental behaviour. And Yoka Daishi was himself a fine model of that very teaching which he bequeathed to us.

The same teaching is derived from the lotus flower, the flower that blooms in water. If it is brought too near to fire, it immediately withers. So fire is the worst enemy of the lotus. Nevertheless, that lotus which blossoms within the range of fire, has a greater and more delicious scent, and is the more beautiful the nearer it gets to that fire. So, too, the person who — like the ordinary lotus which sees fire as its greatest enemy — avoids and dislikes the 'five lusts' and comes to meditation obsessed with the danger of them, and even though that person might be well informed about the 'two voids' — that neither self nor life has any reality — and no matter how clear might be his knowledge and discernment — if he should leave the calm of meditation and go out into the fire, or life of activity, he will be like a shellfish or leach which has no water, or a baboon or monkey separated from its forest trees. He will not have the vitality, not even half the vitality, he should have. That person will, in fact, be like the lotus blossom which instantly withers when it is brought near to fire.

If, on the other hand, one remains amongst the ordinary 'six dusts' of active life, and clothes oneself with a sort of spiritual sheen, is simple, unalloyed, complete and of one piece, that person will not err to any great degree. He may be compared to the man in the story who delivered that treasure of gold whilst passing through great riots and disturbances of the worldly life. He is one who boldly and successfully displays his courageous disposition and advances without delay or hesitation. And by the very fact of so doing, such a man raises up the very source and origin of his own mind, and brings to a final end all those roots of existence which tie him to the cycle of birth and death. For a person like that, there is nothing but great joy, enough to dissolve the sky and shatter the iron mountains. He is to be compared with the lotus which blossoms and becomes ever more beautiful and more deliciously scented as it gets nearer to fire. And if you ask, 'How can this be?' It is because the fire is itself the lotus, and the lotus is itself the fire.

What I wish to do here is to repeat — and it cannot be repeated enough — that this discipline of introspection must not be arbitrarily or excessively indulged in. It is truly essential that proper care be taken in the matter.

The true discipline of introspection teaches us to realise that the 'inexpressible, absolute truth' about which Joshu (778-897) wrote, is to be identified with the very elements which we see in our own selves, in our own bodies.

The true practice of introspection is, to this mind of mine, below the navel, the breathing centre of the abdomen and the loins and feet, and is in totality the 'no' ideogram *(mu)* of Joshu, i.e. the inexpressible reality. And what logical reasoning is there in that? This mind of mine below the navel, the breathing centre of the abdomen and the loins and feet is in totality my own personal dignity, and where is the place for any nostrils in my personal dignity? This mind of mine below the navel, the breathing centre of the abdomen and the loins and feet, is in totality my one and only Pure Land — and what grandeur is there in this Pure Land? This mind of mine, below the navel, the breathing centre of the abdomen and the loins and feet is in totality the Amida Buddha of my body, and this Amida — what dharma does he expound? This mind of mine below the navel, the breathing centre of the abdomen and the loins and feet is in totality the home of my origin — what need is there of news of my home?

Coughing, spitting, using the writing brush, awake or asleep — can any resolve of such a man be left unattained or unaccomplished? If he, without delay, stirs up his determination and courageous will, what his ordinary will and consciousness could not do, with unexpected, unearned freshness of heart, with unexpected clarity — as one who can walk over ten thousand miles of ice, and could equally advance into the midst of a rebel camp or step onto the stage of a theatre — he will be as if he were in a place where no man is — he will be like King Kiu mentioned by Ummon whose great mental activity will issue forth and proclaim itself.

Then all the buddhas and all sentient beings will be but illusions. Life, death, nirvana will be but dreams. Heaven and hell will be seen through. The Buddha-world and the demon's palaces, will vanish and melt away. At his own volition he will expound the tiniest mysteries of the million immeasurable 'dharma-gates'. He will bring blessings to all existences.

He will never be exhausted even though passing through innumerable hindrances. He will never be poor in his long and careful 'spiritual alms rounds' (i.e. in his efforts to bring enlightenment to others). He will clear up the ten thousand deeds of illusionary vision (literally the deeds which cause effects and appear to those of misted eyesight like flowers in the sky). He will establish passages through the valley of sounds (i.e. this world of form and sound).

Kwai-so (c. 660) of the Sei-hei temple was a great man far surpassing ten thousand others. He was in a state of calm and quiet, and safety. He had a mysterious consciousness and vision, but the crowd of watchers had no vision, and thought it sufficient to polish and purify their minds. One can hardly believe even in a dream, that there could be such people.

This crowd, day by day practise not being caught up in phenomena, and yet all day long they are caught up in it. All day long they aim at the infinite but are up against the finite. And why is this? Their insight is not clear. To them the dharma-nature of reality is uncertain. They are to be pitied because, as regards this life which is so hard to come by, they enter like a blind tortoise going into an empty valley, or they guard a coffin like a ghost. They pass through life in darkness and return uncorrected to their home of the three hells (the lower realms of the Wheel of Life).[12] All of this is because they had received bad guidance, and the root of their 'vision' was not true. As a result, the toil of their heart-energy was wasted, and they were unable to obtain even the slightest merit. They are truly to be pitied.

The priest Ippen Shonin (1229-1289) of the Ji sect (Ji-shu), hung a gong round his neck and went up and down the country chanting the name of Amida Buddha *(Namu Amida Butsu)*, and continually bewailed the errors of people as he told them: 'If once you enter the threshold of the lower realms, there can be no second return.' Giving this warning, he travelled eastwards to the provinces of Oshu and Dewa, and westwards to the furthest parts of Hakata in Tsukushi, and he visited the founding priest of the temple of Yura,[13] where it is said he finished his great work as a bodhisattva and entered nirvana. Are not his footsteps to be highly valued?

When one thinks carefully about the beginning and ending of this world of ours in which we exist, it is evident that the power of wealth is not enough to enable people to be born into the heavenly realms, nor are works of wickedness worth mentioning as sufficient to cause them to drop down into the hell states, because ultimately it is life in this corrupt world which inspires all these. Those in this world who have attained to such high positions as that of kingship or ministries of state, or who are the great ones of the earth, or who are just ordinary laypeople, obtained some merit in past lives which has enabled them to attain to the positions they hold in this world. They have sown the seeds of good karma triumphing over evil deeds, but their 'wealth' was not enough for them to be born into the heavenly realms. They have merely succeeded in being born into homes of wealth and abundance. They have retainers and concubines surrounding them; and they have heaps of property which they control, but they do not have true discernment. Therefore, they are not benevolently disposed towards the common people, and do not show kindness to children. The only thing that is great about them is their love of luxury. Today they perform evil works which bring evil karmic effects; and tomorrow they cause pain or even commit murder. They have come into this world bearing a certain amount of virtue, but they vainly set up for themselves a glory which is nothing but a mirage in the sky. Burdened by an endless repetition of evil works, they will return to the eternal city of evil; and there seems to be no end to this sort of evil in this world. That is why I repeat again to you that you should not overlook the essential secret of correct introspection, but should practise it constantly.

Now, first of all, in this discipline of introspection, there is the secret art of nourishing life itself. Introspection is in accord with what the hermits call the 'elixir of life'. This art began with the sage, Chin-hsian (Konsen Shi). Later it reached Chisha, founder of the Tendai School, who gave minute information about it in his *Mahashikwan Sutra*. I, myself, heard about it in the middle of my life from my teacher, Hakuyu. Hakuyu concealed himself in a cave near Shirakawa, in the province of Yamashiro. I was told that he had passed 240 years in review during his life. The local people used to call him 'the hermit Hakuyu'. He is said to have been the first teacher of Jozan Shi (Ishikawa Jozan, 1583-1672).

Hakuyu said about this matter: 'The art of life-nourishment consists in keeping the upper parts of the body cool, and the lower parts warm. It is essential to know that for the nourishing of life, one should concentrate one's vital energy in the lower parts. People who hear that the divine elixir is only a matter of practising the five good works (alms, meditation, etc.), do not know that the five basic elements which make up the material body (fire, wood, metal, water and earth) are known by the five sense organs (eye, ear, nose, tongue, touch). If somebody asks what is meant when it is said that the kneading of the elixir is performed by "assembling" all the five roots or senses of the body, it must be answered that there is the law of the five elements which prevent the increasing of desire. The eye, for instance, must not look at random; the ear must not listen at random; the tongue must not talk at random; the body must not touch at random; nor must the mind think at random. When these important laws are adhered to, the spirit of this complex essential nature will be supplied, as it were, before one's very eyes. This essential nature is what Mencius called "the expansive spirit". From this it follows that by concentrating this vital energy in the space below the navel and preserving it year after year so that it becomes invincibly strong, then before you realise it, the elixir-oven will raise the elixir (the outer, the inner, and the central), and the eight regions and the four quarters of the universe will become one great elixir-confection. Then one will realise that one's self has not come to birth before heaven and earth, and that one's self does not die later than the Void, but that one is oneself, a divine hermit having length of life. With this attainment comes the power to stir up the great ocean into cream, and to change the hard soil into harder gold; and so it is said that "one grain of the elixir changes iron into gold"'.

Haku-o said, 'It is essential to nourish life.' This is not just moulding the form. The secret of moulding the form involves discipline tempering the spirit. When the spirit is disciplined, the mind becomes concentrated. When the mind is concentrated, the elixir is produced. When the elixir is produced, the form becomes fixed, and when the form is fixed, the spirit is perfected. It should be known that the elixir is certainly not an outward thing, an outward object.

We know that there are jewel fields and millet fields in the earth. Jewel fields are places where jewels are produced, and millet fields are places where grain plants are grown. So too, in man there is what we call the 'space below the abdomen' and this is the treasure room where energy is stored and preserved. This is the fortress town where the divine elixir is purified so that life may be preserved for long years. There is an ancient saying that an arm of the sea can control a hundred valleys because it descends to a great depth. The ocean itself already occupies ten thousand waters underneath, so even though it enfolds one hundred rivers, the ocean itself never increases nor diminishes in size. So, too, the lower abdomen has its position underneath the five internal organs of the body. It never tires of storing up the energies. And when the divine elixir has been produced and perfected, it enters into the hermit city. This elixir is itself in three places, but the elixir I am speaking of is in the lower one. The elixir place and the lower abdomen are both below the navel; they are one thing with two names. The elixir place is two inches below the navel. The point in the abdomen (where energy comes from) is an inch-and-a-half lower. And the true energy is always preserved within these. When the mind and body are even, then though life may be long and see one hundred years, the hair will not dry up, the teeth will not get loose, the eyesight will be clear, and the skin will gradually become lustrous. This is the experience when the energy has been preserved and the divine elixir perfected. There will be no end to the counting of the years.

But, of course, the efficacy of this discipline depends entirely on how purely or how coarsely it is performed. The physicians of ancient times who dealt with the mind used to heal before the disease began. They made people control their minds and attend to their spirit. The ordinary run of modern physician does just the opposite. After seeing the disease which has already taken hold, they try to cure it by the three methods of acupuncture, moxacautery and potions. Many are not saved. For it is a matter of fact that soul, mind and spirit, are the three foundation pillars of the self. So the wise man is careful to attend to his mind and not waste it.

To put the matter another way: The art of preserving life may be compared to the art of protecting a country. What we call the 'spirit' is like the prince; what we call the 'soul' is like a minister of state; and what we call the 'mind' is like the people of the land. Just as loving the people is the means of perfecting the state, so being careful as to how one attends to the soul and mind is the means of perfecting the body. When the people are squandered away, the country perishes. When the 'mind' is exhausted, the body dies. That is why a sagely prince puts his own heart (desires) at the bottom. The ordinary sort of prince, however, attends selfishly to his own heart (desires), And when he selfishly attends only to the top, he relies on the 'nine lords' of high estate, preens himself on having under his authority the 'hundred officials' but never gives thought to the poverty and decay of the common people. Then avaricious ministers rob, and exacting officials deceive and flay the poor. In the fields there is a look of starvation and men fall down from starvation. Then the wise and the good dive into concealment. Between the officials and the people there arises anger and envy, until at last the common people are reduced to the greatest misery, and the pulse of the nation ceases to beat.

But when the attention of the ruler's desires is given sincerely to the lower classes, and the labour and weariness of the people is never forgotten, then the people become prosperous and the whole country becomes strong. No officials rebel. No enemies invade the land.

So it is with one's body. Wise and sensible people always keep their heart-energy low down. And for that reason the 'seven ills' do not find a place in which to move about, nor can the 'four false views' invade them from without. The defences are protected, and so the inner forces — the mind and spirit — are preserved in health; and the body does not have to undergo the pains of acupuncture or moxacautery. Such a body is like a powerful nation which does not have to listen to the sound of war drums.

Long ago the sage, Gi-Haku, replied to a question by the Yellow Emperor Huangdi (legendary Emperor, 4,000 BC) by saying: 'If there is inward calm, void within, then the mind conforms.' If one protects the inner spirit, from where can illnesses come? Today, unfortunately, people do the opposite. From the time of their birth until their death, not for a single moment does the mind protect their inner self. They do not even know what this ruling mind of theirs is! They merely run about following their own feet. How dangerous! Is it not said in the homes of the warriors that it is because this ruling mind is not properly fixed that unexpected distresses arise. Surely it is evident that when the mind protects the inner self, distresses will not come at random. Even if it is for just one minute, if in anyone there is no ruling mind, such a person does not differ in any respect from a dead man. At any rate, it cannot be said that profligacy will not beset such a one.

Say, for example, there is an old house dwelt in solely by an aged woman. There she is — decrepit, emaciated and in the extremity of weariness and starvation. Still, no stranger would enter that place without reason, not even if that woman was absent. When that house loses its owner, however, burglars break in and even rest there; beggars hide in it and sleep there; foxes and rabbits run about in there; and badgers hide in there. There might also be wandering ghosts heard crying out and moaning there in the daytime. A thousand suspicious things, a hundred ghost-like forms might be there. Altogether it might well become the cave-dwelling of crowds of evil beings. And so it is with a person's body.

When it is as if all were settled immovably and persistently like a rock in the lower abdomen, not one jot of illusory thought, not an atom of desire or lust, or half a pint of mantic desire, would be found there. At that point, heaven and earth would be at one's command. The universe would be the steed upon which one rides. One would be a keen performer of the discipline, as hard and firm as Mount Koju, and like the merciful and benevolent ocean itself. Buddha himself could not insert his hands against such people, nor could demons spy on them. Day after day those people could perform ten thousand good works without becoming weary. They would be called truly grateful sons and daughters of the Buddha.

If, however, people are captivated suddenly by evil conditions, drawn away by wanton conditions without realising it, they may lose the power of control. This is called 'sudden ignorance'.[14] It is a state in which thoughts are created, names are made up, and activities begin. Then evil demons of hindrances rise up like bees round them and be-witching spirits bringing false views hustle about them like ants. The decaying house of the four elements of dreams and hallucinations, the home of the five hindrances and imaginary flowers in the sky, is immediately changed and becomes the dwelling of demons.

There are thousands of forms, ten thousand appearances. Every day tens of thousands of kinds of life and death are here. Outwardly, perhaps, it might look like the shape of a high-stepping gentleman, but in the inner heart the changes of mind which take place are as many as those of the very devil! In such a mind there is more pain eternally present than there was in that terrible battle of Yashima. Within that breast are greater disturbances than there were in the rebellion of the 'nine nations'. One thinks of the story of the conflagration in the rich man's house (in the parable told us in the *Saddharma Pundarika)*. Such a mind is known as the 'sea of karma' in which birth and death are perpetually rising and sinking. And if there is no raft there, no true raft of meditation on reality, and no sailing ship of bold and brave ascetic discipline, then that unruly mind will be drawn down into the swift current of the waves of vain knowledge and whirling desire. And such a mind will never be able to pass safely through the evil-smelling and poisonous fog of darkness, to reach the farther shore of the four virtues.[15]

Alas! Alas! People of this sort, may be equipped with the wisdom and virtues of humanity, and with the marvellous state of the Tathagata with nothing lacking; they may be provided with the 'cintamani jewel'[16] which can fulfil every wish of the possessor; they may have the jewel of buddha-nature; they may perpetually radiate the bright light[17] of the bodhisattva body; they may be dwelling in the land of purity where this world of suffering is identical with that buddha-world where eternal truth is revealed, or in that land of Vairocana where dharma-nature and the absolute are manifest; and yet, in spite of these wondrous states — because their 'wisdom eye'[18] has been blinded — they look at all these marvellous truths in a perverted way. They can only see it all as part of the world of suffering; they think of it all as being nothing but sentient existence in darkness; they have no real discrimination; they expend their human bodies which are so hard to come by in the cycle of karma lives; they waste their human lives; they just go round and round wandering in the city of the 'three hells' which were so painful to them in the past, and in the 'six regions' of the Wheel of Life[12] which are so miserable for them all; they grasp at the unchanging land of Vairocana's eternal calm, yet in their minds fear that it is itself hell; and they weep as if it were the lowest of the hell realms, the Avici hell itself. Such is the way of the world — an insignificant boasting in small indecisive views. It is a boasting in painfully ridiculous learned explanations which come through the senses (ears and mouths). It shows a disbelief in the Buddhadharma, a deafness to the true dharma, a one-sided efficacy which does not for one moment protect the right thinking of the mind. Greatly to be pitied, and evermore pitied, is that eternal transmigration. To be feared and evermore feared are the painful fruits of the long night of life and death.

It is said, even of the emperors of the Enki and Tenryaku eras (898-930 and 947-967) — emperors who were revered as 'three sages of the world' — that they were seen by Nichizo Shonin (d. 985) being blackened and scorched in the fierce fires of the sixth hell state. These emperors said to Nichizo: 'Because we relied on the fact that we were rulers of Japan (the little kingdom shaped like dispersed millet) and therefore lived in luxury and pride, we have become what you now see us to be.' So too with Fujiwara no Toshiyuki Ason who was distinguished for his genius both in China and Japan, and famous for his beautiful handwriting, and who copied out two hundred volumes of the *Saddharma Pundarika Sutra*. Because he did not possess the right spirit of meditation in his life, he dropped into the painful hell realms and went to Tomonori of Ki-i and begged to be helped and delivered. Or again, it is said that even Hachiman-dono (Minamoto no Yoshiie), that famous warrior who was called the 'Unrivalled General of the Imperial Court', who set the Emperor's heart at ease at a time when all the incantations of high-ranking priests of the Southern City and the Northern Capital had wearied the Emperor's brain, by scratching and wiping them off the face of the earth with the mere sound of his bowstrings. As a result, this great Hachiman-dono had to kneel in the outer porch of the king of hell, Enma. And the famous Tada Manju during an illness was once called, we are told, by a messenger of the king of hell, Enma, and shown the sights of the city of darkness. When he returned to life he was so terrified by what he had seen that he immediately entered the 'six-sided temple'[19] in Kyoto and began studying the buddha-way, reciting prayers to Buddha. It is said that his tears and sweat poured through the very straw mats on which he was sitting. So, too, King Sojo of Ts'in (Chuang-hsiang of the Ch'in, d. 247 BC) who annexed the Six Lands, united the Four Seas, and was feared as far as the bounds of the Barbarian States, fell into a state of hell where he suffered terrible pains. Also, Hakki (Peh-chi) of Ts'in, received punishment from Emperor Wu of Sung. He became known throughout the whole world as a terrible villain, and sank into a hell state of filth and slime. At the beginning of the reign of the Ming Emperor Ko-Bu, (Hong-u) (1638), Hakki was seen at a place called the 'Place of the Three Reed Vision' on Mount Go-u (Kiang-su Province). An enormous white centipede over a foot long was killed by a bolt of lightning, and people saw inscribed on its back a large ideogram, 'Hakki', which was the ancient villain's name! This shows how difficult it is for people to escape from their own evil karmic chains.

Do not, therefore, say that there is no time to meditate, that there is too much business, and that it is almost impossible to carry on one's plans for meditation when the duties of this world are so pressing. It should be known that for a robed monk who meditates in the right spirit, there is no such thing as business, or worldly affairs.

Supposing a man drops two or three money bills in a street where there is a great deal of traffic and crowds of people. Will he leave it there because there are so many eyes watching him, or because there is so much traffic? Surely not! It is more likely, he will push his way through the crowd and will not be easy until he has got the lost money back into his own hands. And what about those who neglect their meditation discipline and forsake their plans to carry on with it properly because, they say, business is too great, and worldly affairs need too much attention? Are they not putting a greater value on two or three pieces of gold than on the sublime and wondrous Way of all the buddhas? If one with total concentration studies the Way, even in the midst of one's business and amongst the waves of the world until one comes to enlightenment, then one will be more like that person who dropped the gold but gave his full attention to finding it again. Having done so, who would not lift up one's eyes with joy?

And that is why Shuho Myocho (1281-1337) said: 'See how, even in horse racing when the colts are running backwards and forwards, even there, meditation can be performed.' And the abbot of Shinju-an said, 'Do not read the sutras — meditate. Do not sweep the garden — meditate. Do not plant tea seeds — meditate. Do not ride a horse — meditate.' This is indeed the ancient truth about right meditation. My own old teacher, Shoju, always used to say: 'Anyone who desires to learn how to meditate uninterruptedly, even if he has to enter a city of murderers and swords, or go into a room of weeping and wailing, or attend a wrestling match, or a theatre or music hall, need not add adjustment of thought to adjustment of thought, nor does he have to make careful calculations about it. All he has to do, is bundle every one of these things into a meditation topic, then go forward without a break and without withdrawing or retreating.'

For instance, supposing the chief demigod of the Asuras were to seize someone by the elbow and force him to go round the three thousand great universes for a thousand of their cycles or a hundred of their revolutions, and supposing that man did not even then lose his correct meditative composure but continued steadfastly, such a person would be a true meditator. There is an ancient saying: 'During the twelve hours of the day, just keep your head cool and your eyes steady and do not let yourself get mixed up with the worldly lusts of mankind.' This is a truly valuable saying. The same truth is told in military law: 'Both fight and cultivate! This is the best of all the ten thousand plans for the warrior.' The same is also true for meditation. Activity is the true discipline for fighting, and introspection is essential for cultivation. These two things are like the two wings of a bird, or the two wheels of a cart.

I wrote about the secret of introspection in my *Yasen Kanna (Chat on a Boat in the Evening)*, and I did so for the benefit of monks during one of their rainy season retreats. I do not know how many were helped in their meditation sickness by what I said, but I do know that eight or nine who were very ill and near to death were cured. Let all who study with regard to the discipline of meditation, store up and compare together the method of introspection and meditation, for they will thereby be able to fulfil the main purpose of their normal lives.

If students of the Way were convinced of the great teachings of the five schools of thought[20] and the seven currents[21] of illusion and how to prevent them, yet only live for a very short time, what would they be able to accomplish? On the other hand, even if, owing to the power of introspection, a vigorous patriarch was to pass in review a period of eight hundred years, but did not possess the 'eye of discernment' he would merely be like a ghost watching corpses. Of what benefit would that be? Or, again, if someone sat in meditation until he was decrepit and was absorbed solely in the silent clarity of mind, he would merely be frittering away his life in a mistaken idea, and would greatly stray from the Buddha's Way.

And why? If all princes were to neglect their morning audiences and give up their state duties in order to sit in long meditation, and if warriors were to be careless about archery practice and forget their military arts in order to sit long in meditation, and if merchants were to close up their shops and break up their abacuses to sit long in meditation, and if farmers were to throw away their spades and ploughs and cease from their cultivation to sit long in meditation, and if artisans were to throw away their inked strings, adzes and axes to sit long in meditation, the whole country would languish, the people would become weary, bandits would be multiplied, and the nation would be in danger. Then the common people would become angry and resentful, and would say that meditation was an unpropitious and ill-omened practice. But it is well known that in ancient times when the Zen teaching was flourishing, all the sagely patriarchs — men like Nangaku Ejo (677-744), Baso (Ma-tsu, 709-788), Hyakujo Ekai (720-814), Obaku (d. 850), Rinzai (d. 867), Kisu Chijo, Ma-goku, Ko-ge (d. c. 900), Banzan, Kyu-bo, and Jizo — used to haul stones, move soil, carry water, cut firewood, peel vegetables, and in this way beat the hand-drum of carpentry and construction work, and thus earnestly seek the attainment of inward strength within the 'way of activity'. And didn't Hyakujo say: 'One day without work, one day without food!' Their activity in the Way is ceaseless meditation. Unfortunately, this method of the ancient patriarchs has been banished from the face of the earth in our modern times. It has ceased.

But what I have just said does not mean, of course, that meditation is to be disliked, or that quiet thought is to be spoken of as evil. There is not so much as one half a wise or holy person of understanding — whether in ancient or modern times — who has not brought the buddha-way to fruition without meditation. The three essentials — morality *(shila)*, meditation, and intelligence (wisdom) — are a summary of the whole of the Buddha's ancient Way. Who can treat these lightly? If people, like all those ancient sages of the meditative way, were to doubt the transcendent and surpassing quality of the true and great way of meditation, then indeed thunderbolts would fall and the stars would be shaken out of the heavens.

But, if one's eyes are only the eyes of sheep, and one's wisdom is only the wisdom of badgers, how can one expect to understand? Supposing that sitting in silent meditation actually does cause one to immediately attain buddhahood and to instantly shed forth the bright light of the bodhisattva mind and body, how is it possible to expect princes, great men, soldiers and people with a thousand duties in their homes to find leisure enough to sit in meditation for even a few minutes? And so people speak of being ill and weary in their public duties, give up their home affairs, and for three, five or seven days they close their doors, fasten the bolts, pile up cushions to sit or lie on, set up sticks of incense and sit meditating. But though they do all that, they get tired from their normal work, and so they only sit meditating for an inch and go to sleep for an ell! And for three pints of meditation they actually collect a million gallons of idle thoughts, because no sooner have they settled their eyes, gritted their teeth, clasped their hands and taken up the correct straight posture for sitting in meditation, than ten thousand wicked states grow up in their heads and compete for their minds. Then they furrow their brows and begin to weep and grieve, saying, 'Our official duties hinder us from performing our meditative practices. Our private way obstructs our contemplation.' Then they resign from their official work, hand in their seals and go to some uninhabited spot, a calm and quiet place near the edge of a stream or under some big tree, and there carry on their meditation in their own self-willed way, hoping thus to escape from the long cycle of transmigration. It all ends in misery!

Really, the way of the retainer is to prepare his lord's food and arrange his clothes, tie his girdle and attach his sword. He does not fetch water from afar. He eats food without cultivating it. He wears clothes without weaving them. His very body — his hands, feet, hair, teeth — all these are benefits provided by his lord. But when he has grown up and is thirty or forty years old, and the time has come for him to repay his lord's kindness by making himself pre-eminent as his assistant, so that his lord may become like those lords of China's Golden Age (Gyo and Shun and people like that), if instead he begins to tell his beads secretly behind his sleeve, repeat Buddha prayers in a low inaudible voice, and becomes languid and careless about public affairs, he has no sense of gratitude for the benefits he has received from his lord, and as likely as not, he says he is sick and retires from duty altogether. But if that is his intention, even if he then disciplines himself in meditation for three or five years in retired spots, and even if he thinks that his thoughts are ceasing and his lusts are coming to an end, he will find that his inner organs are twisted and painful, and that there are still many fears in his heart, so that even if he so much as hears the droppings of a mouse, his bosom will burst.

Whether he was a general or a private soldier, what special duty would such a man be fit for? Supposing some great crisis came upon the land. If it were only men like that who could go out to reinforce some exposed gate of the castle when the enemy was rushing up to it like a great tide of the sea — flags and banners waving like clouds all round, cannon balls falling about in every place like lightning, terrible roarings and re-echoings of noise taking place, bells ringing and reverberating as if the very mountains were falling, and spears and lances shining like icicles out in the battle lines — if there were only men like that who saw and heard such things, they would not be able to swallow for fear, their hands would tremble so much they would not even be able to seize hold of the hand-ropes. On horseback they would squat on the saddle, holding on as if they were about to fall off on account of their own trembling. At last they would be taken prisoner by foot soldiers! And why should all this happen? It would be because they sat in silence and calm with emaciated looks for three or five years in so-called meditation. Why, even such great heroes as Kumagai or Hirayama, if they were to carry on that sort of meditative discipline, would surely tremble.

The patriarchs in their compassion and goodness pointed to the correct way to right thought and activity, and uninterrupted meditation. If princes have the right spirit of meditation when they are giving their morning audiences, and if the retainers have the right spirit of meditation when they are practising their archery or performing their literary and business duties, and if farmers, likewise, have the right spirit of meditation when they are using their ploughs and spades, and artisans have that spirit when they are using their inked-strings and axes, and women have that same spirit when they are sewing and weaving, then they would all of them be carrying out the practice of the 'great meditation' as taught by the holy ones. And that is what is meant by the scripture which says that 'property, life, production, and labour — none of these are opposed to reality'.

If, however, there is not correct meditation activity, then everything is like an old badger sleeping in an empty hole. It is very sad that people today are casting off the Way and becoming nothing better than the dust of the earth. More often than not, nowadays, people are unable to recognise the black, dark valley of the two voids — of the self and of the dharma — but think it to be the sublime end of meditation. Every day they frown and furrow their brows and are no better than silkworms in their cocoons. The patriarchs are separated from them by clouds and smoke! Their dislike of the sutras is like an injured mouse trying to escape from a cat. Their abhorrence of the patriarchal records reminds one of a dying hare listening to the growls of a tiger. Especially are they ignorant of the fact that the ancient hole into which the two lower grades of beginners are always falling is very like nirvana! Even the sage Shuho Daishi (1281-1337) said: 'I myself for three years lived in a foxhole, that many people are often deluded is reasonable,' and he heaved a great sigh! And Prince Ko composed a poem in which he said: 'The captured fish stays in its bowl; the sick bird lives in its cage. They know a little peace, but do not know the great peace.'

But with regard to the upper grades of learners of the true mysteries, in their case it is only a matter of how deep or shallow their entry is into reality, a matter of how pure or coarse their efforts are to reach discrimination. Who shall choose whether one shall stay in one's own home or renounce the world? Who shall argue as to whether one should stay in the busy city or go into the mountain forests?

In the old days there were many great men, like Kobi of Sagami, Rikko of Tai-fu, Tohi Riko, Yoko Tainen, Choko Mujin, who could discriminate the real nature of things as easily as they could look at the palm of their own hands. Their meditation came out of their lungs and inward parts. They trod on and churned up the very depths of the buddha-sea. They swallowed the bitter waters of the waves of the river of Zen. They were as honourable as mirrors of wisdom. They were magnanimous in the weight of their cognition of the truth. Idle spirits fled from them in fear;

field ghosts trembled before them in distress. But all of them gave their assistance in state affairs, and so helped to bequeath peace to the world. They put the world into the peace of Mount Tai. Who can look into the inmost sanctuary of their own minds?

A man like Choko, for instance, rose to be assistant Minister of State and reached the highest grade of officialdom. Rich was his genius as Minister. He was trusted by his prince, honoured by other ministers, revered by warriors, and the common people clung to him. Heaven rained down plenteousness. His prince gave him many titles of honour. He lived to be nearly a hundred, and his radiance flowed out to four seas. The people prided themselves with the autumn fruits of this era of Gyo. Men assumed the liveliness of the days of Shun. They felt gratitude towards their prince. And above all, the treasure of the dharma was quietly preserved. Truly, he was a great figure in the world! And it used to be said too of Cho Mujin: 'He who lives in his home and practises the Way, is Cho Mujin. He who lives in his home and obtains merit, spreads the inexhaustible Way *(tao)*. And for him who eats his own rations and perfects Zen, his years are as the willow.' Will not these beautiful words last for a thousand years?

And then there are people such as Naikan, Ko Rochoku, Cho Shisei, Cho Tengaku, Kwaku Kobo and many others of whom we have no records or traditions. Indeed, there is no limit to their numbers! In their performance of the Way, each of these people have excelled those who meditated under trees. On countless occasions they have assisted in public business; they have attended ceremonial affairs of many lands; they have stood in splendid throngs of officials wearing the 'silver fish' and 'golden turtle' insignias of office. They have been present at ceremonial musical entertainments and archery tournaments, and have been in attendance at imperial abdications and retirements. But they have never for one instant interrupted their practise of the Way. Finally, they penetrated through to the mystery of the patriarchs. Was not this due to their spiritual experience of uninterrupted Zen, their activity of right thought? Was this not the deep goodness of the wondrous Way of the Buddha? Was this not the unique and glorious merit of the patriarchs?

Truly, there is the difference of heaven and earth between these people and the sort of people who think it sufficient to sit in emaciated meditation, dying of starvation on hills and in valleys, and regarding such deathly calm to be the 'root' Zen! Are they not people who, as the saying goes, 'not only fail to catch the hare but lose the falcon too?' It is not only that they have been unable to attain to real discernment, but they have even ceased in the other duty of feeling gratitude to their lord. They are to be greatly pitied. It should be known that everything depends on the energy put into it, and whether the intention is to truly progress or not. If there is energy sufficient to fight ten thousand men, then why should one need to choose between the forest or the home? If final discernment comes only to the men of the forest, then would all hope be lost for those who are parents, retainers, or children living in the world? Supposing one is living the 'forest' life — if that person's religious spirit is not minutely ordered and careful, and if his thoughts are not kept pure — in what way is that different from life in a house? And, conversely, if someone is a householder and has a strong aspiration for discernment, is wise and sincere in his daily work, what difference is there between that and living in the forest? And that is why it is said: 'If the Way is deep down in the mind, it is not necessary to live on Mount Yoshino.' So, at any rate, the meditation planned for by officials, will not excel the uninterrupted Zen of true thought. This is an ancient truth which has been forgotten for the past two hundred years.

Now, if asked, 'What is this spirit of meditation?' I reply that it is to have a sincerely benevolent and sympathetic heart at all times, whether one is talking or writing, moving or resting, whether one's luck is good or bad, whether one is in honour or in shame, in gain or in loss, or in the right or in the wrong, and to do this by bundling up all these things into one verse heading and concentrating your energy with the force of an iron rock under the navel and lower part of the abdomen. Be kindly disposed towards your lord as chief object of reverence. Regard the great officials as your own associates, as a company of illustrious bodhisattvas. Regard the ministers of state, whether they are attendant on the lord or residing at a distance, as being members of the company of disciples of the two lower orders (*shravakas* and *pratyekabuddhas*), as men who have been led to the Buddha by Shariputra and Maudgalyayana. And look upon all ordinary warriors and common people as if they were your own children being instructed in the Way.

If you have this spirit, then your very clothes, your divided skirt *(hakama)* and your upper robes *(kataginu)* will be to you as the seven-pieced robe, or the nine-folded stole *(kesa)* of monks. Your two-edged sword will be your desk or meditation table, placed always before you. Your saddle will be the cushion on which you sit in meditation. The hills, the streams, the plains, will be the floor of your meditation hall. The four corners of the earth and its ten directions, the height and the depth of the universe, will be to you the great cave in which you meditate. They will be, in very truth, the substance of your real self. Then the positive and negative principles of creation will be to you your two daily meals of gruel. Heaven, hell, the Pure Land, and this impure world will be your internal organs (your spleen, stomach, liver and kidneys). Then the hall of the arts with its outer and inner courts of three hundred mats where state business takes place, will become the morning and evening meetings of instruction and scripture-reading. The trillions of Mount Sumerus[22] will be, as it were, bundled together to become your spinal column, and every form of activity in the world of affairs, such as abdication ceremonies, retirements of lords, archery meetings and writing up accounts — all of these will become to you the wondrous works of the good purposes of the bodhisattvas. They will draw forth the heart of brave and bold men; they will bring you into harmony with that true discipline of introspection. Then, from time to time, whether standing or sitting, moving or resting, test whether you have lost the right spirit or not. This is the way of the true discipline of the wise and holy ones of past and present.

This is a matter of uninterrupted meditation in all activities of life. The sage said: 'The Way must not be departed from even for a short time. What may be departed from is not the Way.' Confucius said: 'When you feel flurried, perform *this* — when you feel hurried, perform *this*.' These words simply mean that the spirit of the Way is never to be lost even for a single moment.

Now, when we speak of the Way, we are speaking of the way of moderation which is taught us in the *Lotus Sutra* (the *Saddharma Pundarika* or *Hokke-kyo*). It is explained to us by such great men as Shikyo Zoji, Jakken Jisha, Gasoku Kanki and all the other Buddhas; and special reference is made to the *Lotus Sutra* because of its teaching about the importance of the correct method of meditation. This method, one must understand, points to the state of the real self.

It is not at all easy to entirely put away the affairs of life and death, but if one attends properly to discriminating final reality, it is enough to blind the right vision even of the Buddha. What is of absolute importance is that the two states — activity and calm, order and contrariness, vertical and horizontal — must have the pure, unmixed, complete and whole truth in the forefront. It must be such, indeed, that even if one were surrounded by a thousand, ten thousand people, one would be as if dwelling alone in a wide open space of thousands of miles, and as the ancients said: 'One's ears as if they were deaf; one's eyes as if they were blind.' Thus should it be all the time. This is the time which might be called 'the season of sincere, real, correctness', and the great doubt is actually present. If, when that time comes, you do not go back, but deliberately go forward, then there will come to you such a joy as has not been seen in all the forty years of your life, nor will you have heard anything so joyous. It will be as if you had broken through a great pack of ice, or breached a veritable fortress of precious stones.

Now, if anyone desires to discover whether his discriminative nature is as it should be, pure and not false, or whether one's energy is really pure or coarse for the attainment of spiritual power, then let that person first of all look carefully at this little *gatha* or spiritual poem. It was composed by Fudaishi (497-569). He was converted when out fishing. He used to work with his wife as a farm labourer, as a hired worker. He meditated at night and read the *Lotus Sutra* twenty-one times. Eventually, he was called to the capital of China and became a famous teacher of the

Tendai School. It is good to read his little poem because it shows how, after penetrating through to reality, he changed the nature of his teaching. Prior to that, he had said: 'Before coming to "verse", come to "understanding".' When he had penetrated through, he said: 'Rather than turning first to thought *(mana)* turn to verse.' Now, Fudaishi in his religious poem said: 'Grasping in his empty hand the spade, and riding on his buffalo, the farmer crosses a bridge. It is the bridge which flows away behind him, not the water.' And in another poem he said: 'The lights in the sacred lanterns leap into the outer pillars. The Buddha's "holy of holies" runs out of the temple gate.' (N.B. The lights of the sacred lantern are symbols of those 'things which contain the dharma'. The outer pillars are symbols of mere 'evanescent supports, pillars of dew'). Again in another poem he says: 'If the ox of the province of Kwai eats rice, the belly of the horse in the province of Eki swells.' Or again: 'If Duke Cho drinks wine, Duke Li gets drunk. If you wish to know the truth right away, face the South and see the Northern Constellation.'

Kanganshi (AD 650) composed this poem: 'White waves rise on the green hills, red dust rises at the bottom of the well.'

When anyone has attained to true discernment of reality, these verses can be understood as clearly as one sees the palm of one's own hand. If you cannot understand their inner meaning, do not say you have attained to enlightenment. But even if you are able to penetrate the meaning of verses like these one by one, do not think that that is sufficient.

Patriarch Shuso Daishi said: 'In the morning knit your eyebrows together, but in the evening knit your shoulders together. Myself, what am I?' And Honnu Enjo Kokushi

(Honnu means *'a priori'* and Enjo means 'absolute') said: 'Here is a saying of the sage Hakuju: "There is even a time for rebels to rebel."' Now, when you have meditated on these topics and have not the slightest doubt about them in your own mind, then you may know that you are at one with the Buddha who originated this way of discernment. And what place is there for shame to be called a high disciple of the mystery?

Why indeed? In practising meditation, it is essential that one is clear about the heart-mind of the Buddha. If one can attain to the knowledge of the buddha-heart, surely it is impossible not to realise the meaning of his words. If one has not attained to illumination and the import of the Buddha's words, then that person has not realised buddha-mind. And so it is written in the *Sutra of the Seven Wise Women* that the Buddha said: 'Those of my disciples who are only arhats cannot express the meaning of my words. Only those who are great bodhisattvas are able to do so.' And when we speak of this meaning, to what are we referring? We are referring to that sublime mystery which has been handed down from patriarch to patriarch, from India to Japan. And it was for the purpose of ensuring we fully understand the correct meaning of the Buddha's words that the patriarchs left these sayings which are so hard to penetrate. In this connection, the hermit of Shinju-an said: 'You five hundred arhats of the Tendai School clothe yourselves in the robes of the dharma and go out amongst the people. Inscrutable miracles will surround you, but the wonders which are not transmitted through the patriarchs, are hard, hard!'

In these times of ours, consider well how the divine afflatus has not descended upon us. In our times, men are foolish and do not discriminate. They are like that foolish sort of person who has not vision enough to distinguish jewels from stones, and such people frequently say: 'We ourselves are, indeed, Buddha, so why should we go through all these hard sayings and meditation topics? So long as our hearts are pure, then the Pure Land is pure, and there is no use in perusing all these old records.'

Those who say that sort of thing, are to be considered as having not yet attained, or having attained only in outward word. They have not yet proved, or have proved only in word, not in reality. They are shameless and foolish. If one were to look inwardly at what might be called the rationale of the minds of such people, we shall find only the '*alaya* wisdom', the dark cave of ignorance. They acknowledge the robber distraction and make it their child. All they do is hand down distraction after distraction, and call it 'the wondrous way of the patriarchal succession'. When men like that see people struggling in learning the Way, they do not know that such people are actually pointing directly to perfect and sudden attainment and are the foundation states of the second vehicle.

They do not understand the 'this and that' of upward and aspiring Zen. They are a species of learner *(shravaka)*; and when one investigates point by point what they call 'direct pointing to perfection and sudden attainment', it is just fundamental ignorance which is so criticised in the *Shurangama Sutra (Ryogon-kyo)*. Such men are greatly inferior to real '*shravakas*'; they belittle the wise and holy ones who have found reality through their own efforts. Such false learners are indeed foolhardy. Or, again, there are some who look at an ideogram such as that for 'nothing' *(Mu)* or they look at an 'acorn', and then they falsely imagine things about them which they cannot even feel with their hands or tread on with their feet, and they say that that is the Way of super-penetration — they think that is the Way of meditation. This is a veritable evil custom. It is a disease of meditation which is far advanced and hard to cure. It is confusion carrying on to still further confusion until it has reached the stage of incurability, a transmission of corpse to corpse, a blind discriminating.

But those who are real bodhisattvas of true learning are quite different. They go to meditation and go, and go again and again, even to places to which it is not necessary to go. Reason exhausts itself. Their words come to an end, and their techniques come to an end. They spread out their hands to the limits of the horizon, and when they reach that limit, they rise again as if from the dead until at last they come to the borders of the 'land of peace'. But whatever way one ventures along this way of the secret, bone-shaking, life-taking search — so hard to penetrate, too hard to explain — especially whilst one is still held by the karma of false ignorance and the cycle of life and death, one cannot fail to be alarmed.

Aged and experienced arhats who have reached *samadhi*, always used to knit their brows and say that the Buddha strongly forbade anyone to teach the law of reality whilst they still possessed a heart of karma revolving in life and death. Nevertheless, in spite of such warnings, eight or nine out of ten priests who wander over the land like rain clouds passing back and forth without any fixed abode, talk loudly without any proper knowledge or study, and say all sorts of things about there being no difficulty or doubt concerning the great teachings of the seventeen hundred traditions of light, the model subjects of meditation (koan). Many of these men get very excited. They raise their fists, hit the mats on which they sit, and spit out sounds from their mouths which are supposed to signify inexpressible truths. If one does not take care, one will find that one has come upon a man who does not rely on any discrimination or even have any merit from study or learning. He may even be ignorant of ideograms, stubborn and narrow-minded, without any vision at all. One cannot but ask what the source is from which they have derived their fearful, knavish and inadequate manner of life. Have any of them been to India or China? What have they been in previous times? Let them but go on vociferating as they do; they will at last lose all their 'scent' and voice. Their attainments are not sufficient to be medicine to cure even a toothache.

It is a most deplorable thing that these men who have the qualifications for becoming chiefs and the abilities of divine beings, could, if they spent their energies in meditation, pile up merits. These men who can trace their traditions back to Baso (709-788), Sekito (700-790), Rinzai (d. 867) or Tokusan (781-865) might grow to be cool shade trees for the whole world. Just at the most important time, however, they accept false interpretations having no foundation of tradition in the line of the dharma. And because of this, they say of those whom they see exhausting their spirits in meditation and learning, that they are merely running around enquiring about useless matters; and they laugh at the true enquirers with resounding repetition.

Why, even a little black-robed acolyte, running round the temple, would — if he knit his brows and put his mind to it — assuredly come to understand the dregs of true discrimination which terminates in true attainment, if he once realised the fact of their 'alaya' sense — that dark cave, so dull and so neutral, neither good nor bad, and its dire consequences. And if that is the case with an acolyte, much more might it be so with those who have received their traditions through alien lines. But what are we to say about those who are 'left in the Buddha's hands'? Some of these may have believed at first, but they have become just blind men, neutral, dull and slow, unable even to attain to the headship of secular households, and eventually becoming disliked and rejected by the almsgivers and parishioners of their own temples, going on and on without knowing how to proceed correctly, as has come to be the custom of present-day pilgrims.

Let us turn aside now, and ask how one can reach true enlightenment in the correct way when surrounded by excessive duties and the business of life in the world, and when one is also endangered by the 'seven errors and eight upsets'.[23] For example, suppose a brave warrior is surrounded by enemies on every side. He is carrying a single spear and is seated on a horse with another at his side. His fierce, bold spirit is roused by danger, but he cannot break through by the mere use of his sword or spear. The spirit he is inspired with, is that of those who uninterruptedly clothe themselves with that spirit of meditation. However, he gets no apparent benefit from his meditative spirit. He can hardly move his hand and foot, and all the four directions become to him an impenetrable emptiness or cave of the void. He feels as if his body and soul might melt away into nothingness. But if he proceeds without fear and advances boldly, then at some point the whole power of attainment may come suddenly upon him.

Speaking more generally, the spirit of meditation is the combating of self-willed thinking. It is a combat against the weight of one's feelings; it is a combat against dark and deep sleepiness; it is a combat against the ideas of right and wrong, of activity and quiet, of disorder and regularity. In fact, it is a combat against all forms of the objective world of the senses — the condition which dulls the mind.

By carrying on the combat with enthusiasm in the correct spirit, one may go on until there is an entirely unexpected attainment of enlightenment. For instance, there was that bodhisattva, Yuse, who had transgressed the precepts and could find no place for repentance. All he could do was to disturb his mind with grief. As soon as he had taken the great vow, however, he entered into a state of meditation eliminating his silent griefs, and suddenly enlightenment came to him, as to an arhat who realises that life is not produced by any external power. So too, Ummon Daishi attained enlightenment after he had broken his left leg.

I-zen of Mount Mo suffered from diarrhoea for many days until his body was painful and weary, and death faced him. He took the great vow, sat in meditation and overcame the pain. Before long his intestines rumbled and moved many times, and suddenly his illness was gone as if it had been wiped away. He had reached the point of great attainment.

Tai-en Ho-kwan Kokushi (known as Kaku-en, 1031-1098), a Tendai priest under Fujiwara Yorimichi (the regent of Japan) was expelled by the priests of Enryaku-ji, of which he had been made abbot only three days after his arrival at the temple. He went to the Flower Garden of Glory (the Imperial Palace) and there visited the aged teacher, Ko-san of Shotaku-ji, and told him of his troubles. He was, however, reviled and driven away with blows. He became terribly angry and went into a bamboo grove to meditate. Because it was a very hot day, he sat without a stitch of clothing on him and meditated in weariness. When night came, millions of mosquitoes swarmed onto his naked body and started to devour him. He resisted scratching the terrible irritations, gritted his teeth, clenched his fists and sat on, meditating in a sort of foolish way.

Several times he nearly lost consciousness, but all of a sudden he experienced enlightenment.

In still more ancient times there was the World Revered One who went into the Himalaya mountains and practised his ascetic discipline for six years until he was nothing but skin and bone. His hair, like reeds of grass, hung down below his elbows and knees. And Eka Daishi (487-593), the Second Chan Patriarch in China, cut off his own arm and penetrated through to the origin of selfhood. Gensha (835-908) was once weeping whilst riding on an elephant's back. He fell off and broke his left leg, but he penetrated through to the very bones and marrow of truth. Rinzai had to swallow much bitter criticism. During all that time there was not one patriarch or sage in all the three periods (past, present or future) who did not possess a nature which could discriminate between things. But in these times of ours, people rely only on the self-willed and empty emotions of their own breasts, and think it sufficient to discriminate and understand just the things which lie at their own feet; and that is why they are unable throughout their whole lives to break through the devil's net, or Mara's net of false imaginings. This is the 'little wisdom' which is such an obstruction to bodhisattvas. This 'little wisdom' is embodied by people like these.

It is said that in olden times when Zen was flourishing, great men of the warrior class who set their minds on attaining the correct spirit of meditation, used to take a company of seven or eight robust soldiers, mount fine horses and gallop round busy places like Asakusa and Ryogoku where there were crowds of people, as though they were performing some important business; and they did it on a day of leisure just before they were to retire from public duty. They wanted to see how strong their will and purpose was, and how much concentration or lack of concentration they had, with a view to carrying on their meditative life to perfect attainment. Had they attained sufficient willpower for their purpose during the time of their life of activity in the world?

Shinsaemon Ninagawa, for instance, on his way to the battlefield attained great insight and power. Ota Dokan (founder of the city of Yedo) composed poems whilst leading his men into battle. One aged arhat performed his preparatory practices and finally completed the full course of meditative discipline at a time when packs of wolves were prowling around and even attacking his village. He spent seven nights sitting in vigil at graveyards, because he wanted to find out whether his spirit of meditation was strong enough to remain unbroken even when wolves were sniffing about him, smelling his neck and ears.

Shoku Shonin of Shosha, the sutra copyist, used to sigh because when worldly thoughts were prolific and fertile, his thoughts of the Way were few and light. When he had prolific thoughts about the Way, on the other hand, he found that worldly thoughts were few and light.

When I review all that I have written above and look at it carefully, it seems to me that I have just gone on writing prolifically, merely repeating worldly ideas — just babbling on and writing things that it will be difficult for anyone to comprehend. So perhaps I ought to wag my tail and beg for pity, because there is now nothing left for me in these last days of my life here in this temple of Kokurin-ji, and I am really half dead and half alive, with only a little breath left in my body, and the morning star and the moon are setting for me. It is not my part now to plant myself in the way of obtaining authority, nor is it for me to fish in the worldly waters of fame. All that I now ask for is that I may be able to assist people a little in their higher understanding and the nature of the Way. Perhaps also I may be able to help a little in the way of learning about the infinite vows of the dharma, and in assisting those who are performing the charitable duty of teaching the dharma to others, and trying to hand it on to those who will come after them.

There is a saying that it is easy to get hold of a thousand ordinary soldiers, but difficult to find a good commanding general. So if you can lay hold of even a little in this letter of mine, and with its help, assist and enlarge the higher understanding of your lord, so that his learning of the way of meditation may be brought to perfection, then some waves of this teaching will assuredly overflow and reach the hearts of those whom your lord controls. And if those near to him on his right and left are bathed in these waves of water, then some of the water — even if only the troughs of the waves — will certainly reach all the people in the castle. And further, if those waves bathe the whole castle, then the troughs will go on until they reach all the people throughout the land. And the reason for this is that the heart of one is the heart of a million. At last it would reach the whole world. At the highest level the lord will feel its influence; and below, all the common people will receive much benefit. If this happens, there will be no government to compare with such a one in any other state.

Such is the tiny purpose of this old priest's daily life. If it were not so, why ever should I burn my solitary lamp all night long, or continually rub my tired eyes, and write words of this sort over and over again and send them, even when I have not been asked for them? If you can find anything in this letter which seems at all reasonable, then do not throw it away, but read it through carefully. Then bring yourself into harmony with this secret art of introspection which is a means of preserving life, and so get both your body and spirit into good health. I trust you will then speedily attain to that power which meditation brings, and that you will soon obtain that joy which belongs to the 'land of fulfilment where cause and effect do not operate'.

My second prayer is that, by means of the increased energy which you may obtain through this method of introspection, you may preserve your life as long as did Takenouchi no Sukune, and the child of Urashima. Then, you will be of true assistance to your lord in his management of his estate, and you will be a comfort because of your compassionate heart to the ordinary people on his lands. And in your inward heart you will protect the 'treasure of the dharma', be satisfied even to repletion with the joy of that dharma and the happiness of the meditative life, until you reach the full attainment of the dharma. That is the whole of my thought and purpose for you.

Ever since I reached middle age, I have been of the opinion that there is no better state of life for undertaking meditative discipline, than that of the warrior. A warrior can never, day or night, permit any cowardice or weakness in his body. Whether in his public duties or in his social life he has to be very careful and strict. He must see that his coiffure is properly set, his ceremonial dress (his *hakama* and *haori*) are in good order, and his long and short swords are carefully attached to his girdle. His manners and his every move must be such that his inner spirit, as it were, overflows and is evident to all who meet him. And think of him as he is mounted on a fine and powerful steed advancing against millions of enemies, going forward through their midst as if he were in a great open space without any people there at all. His expression is that of one who will cut through and break down all his foes. That is the bright and clear spirit of meditation. When the warrior goes forth in that spirit, he may attain in one month the spiritual energy which it would take the ordinary person who deliberately leaves the world, a year or more to attain. Whilst one who leaves the world would need a hundred days to acquire a certain amount of spiritual power, such a warrior may have the good fortune to acquire in three days.

Unfortunately, many warriors do not set their minds on acquiring this good fortune, and do not know how such a spirit as this may give them true guidance, so when they are mounted on the black backs of their sleek horses, they all unknowingly pile on forty bushels and twenty gallons — a truly heavy load of ignorance and imagination — and go on their way with forbidding looks and distorted faces, riding after each other and slashing away with their swords wherever they happen to be. Is this not a lamentable habit of the present times? Those people who are passing through places like that where the true spirit of meditation could be preserved so well, say that there is not even a crack of opportunity for them to carry on any meditation because of their official business. Such men can only be likened to those swimming in the ocean and looking for water!

In the *Sutra of Forty-Two Chapters* it says: 'There are twenty difficult things for those who are in exalted and noble positions when it comes to trying to learn the Way.' This is very true. From kings to commoners, there are numberless people who have glory, fame, wealth and honour, but if one were to sweep the world one could not find a single one amongst them all who so feared the painful wheel of ever-revolving life that he set himself to learning the essentials for escaping that cycle of existence. This is the gist of our teaching which does not differ from the views expressed by the golden mouth of the Buddha. How can one expect to find any good karmic results in a world where people only covet wealth and fame and are never satisfied? Nor are they satisfied when they are seeking ever more and more luxury and honour.

Your lord is about the only one who sees wealth and fame as nothing but a 'flower of imagination in the sky'; and who knows that luxury and honour are of a piece with dreams and fantasies. He alone is always bending his mind and turning his thoughts towards the sublime and great Way. Three times he has been so considerate as to visit this old shack of mine. In ancient days Prince Wu did that sort of thing in his ardent desire to learn the Way. He visited the temple of his time when he was planning to combine and unite the three lands of India, China and Japan. But your lord did so because he was seeking to pass beyond and transcend the three worlds (past, present and future) in his desire to reach the farther shore of nirvana. So, though their acts seemed similar, the purpose inspiring them was different.

In ancient times the reply to Prince Wu's three visits was made by the priest throwing away his plough and risking his very life. How, then, can I begrudge a few words in order to reply to the three kind visits made to me by your lord?

I have gone on writing this letter, wondering what is the best exposition of the Way to give, and my words do not satisfy me. But I pray all the time that your lord may raise his brows with joy when he reads them or hears them, and that his spirit may be strengthened. At the same time, I hope that perchance I may help to provide a penetrating insight into the teaching of the dharma. However, this latter business of advancing the teaching of the dharma is not at all the sort of thing that can be done merely by the use of forceful words or letters. What is needed is to keep one's purpose fixed in the direction of practising the spiritual discipline, and then one will conform naturally with the great work.

Your special messenger took up his whip in urgent haste the day before yesterday, before I had time to compose a reply to your letter. I am anxious not to seem remiss in my proper attention to you and your request. Fortunately, yesterday a man named Gizen told me that he was about to return to Ibara, so I was overjoyed because I could delay him in order to bring you this reply. For a whole night I did not sleep, and although — from twilight until dawn — I managed to put together five hundred lines, I do not feel I have put into them all that my heart wished to. In my old age, I find that my memory is feeble. I have written at the end of the letter things which I had already said in the beginning, and repeated many things. Also, there are many circumlocutions and many crooked changes in the lines, but there is no time to go through the letter again, so I am closing it up and am going to place it in Gizen's sleeve-pocket. It is like putting in a chicken of So, calling it the phoenix of the elixir, and sending it to the lord.

When you have given it a lightning glance through, I pray you hand it to some children of grade C or D in intelligence, and then keep it a strict secret. If you do happen to find anything in it to take hold of, however, I will write it all again and present it properly. In that case, please let your lord give orders to some of his secretaries to make three or five copies. Distribute these amongst three or five groups of students who live in the neighbourhood and are young, and also to Wada and his companions. Make them read it sometimes. And on days of leisure, call together the people of filial duty *(koko)*, Tsutsumi, Nakasawa and the old retainer physician, with six or seven older men. Put them together in a room and make them listen to it. The lord himself might perhaps sit on a cushion and doze whilst it is being read. It might help to strengthen his own sentiments about the Way. If half a day of leisure is spent pleasurably in this way, a state of joy in the dharma and happiness in meditation will become very evident to you all. You will not need to envy the Four Heavenly Kings or the happiness of Tori. You will even be beyond envying the world which has triumphed over Yama and his soldiers. Still less will you feel envy of the shameless repletion of the banquets of words, the lightness and luxury of the pleasures of error, the pitiless and shameful hallucinations which make deaf the ears of those who hear the Eight Voices of the Buddha,[24] and blind the eyes of those who dance in the ten thousand dancing halls. It is too marvellous to contemplate!

With this purpose, then, and with great tolerance, you will think of learners — those who are nearby, as well as those who are at a distance — as a great audience of tens of thousands, and entice them; and do this all in accord with the great vow of bodhisattva-hood seeking to become a teacher of the Way to all sentient beings. Then there will come to you the unprecedented robes and crown of true wisdom, even in the midst of the dust of life's business. And none knows if he may not be able to turn the sublime dharma-wheel of all the buddhas, even whilst he continues to wear his sword, is seated on the saddle of his horse, and rides up and down the roads. And then there is that well-known saying: 'Under a strong general there are no weak soldiers.' So it may come to pass that under your banner, numbers of people may appear like those influential warrior retainers: Kishi, Kyoki, Shinshi, Manji and Nomura or Tamura.

Then, if by some chance a great crisis occurs, your general with his soldiers could march out with true vigour and boldness — though but one hundred against ten thousand cavalries — and 'where life has not been seen, how could death be seen!' Such a company would be like the pushing forward of a rock or iron. They would be as calm as a mountain peak; they would be as swift as a hurricane. No place could withstand an assault by such men. No place which they touched would remain unbroken. Even if they found themselves in the midst of the battlefields of the rebellions of the Gempei wars, they would stand firm as if they were in the middle of an uninhabited plain. Their power would be that of determined and bold men. The soldiers they lead would be trained and disciplined by a combination of the sentiments of gratitude to the dharma; and who amongst such men would begrudge his life for the sake of such a lord? And if one has no fears about life or death, there will be no seeking for nirvana. At such times for such people, all ten directions of the universe would melt away into nothingness before their eyes; all the three worlds of past, present and future would become concentrated in one thought. And all this is due to the power which comes from true thinking and the true spirit of meditation.

When such a state of affairs comes about, the warriors are respectful, the people cleave to their lord, the lord is benevolent, and his ministers are just. The farmers have sufficient millet, the women have enough cloth, and all classes of people love the Way. The pulse of the nation is as calm as the peace of Mount Tai. There is no deterioration or diminishing throughout the ten thousand ages; and nothing can be found like the good karmic results anywhere else amongst men or gods. The upper officials attain to true enlightenment, and the acting officers who know the Way, will not behave like aliens!

> With deep respect, the 5th day of the Summer Dragon month of the calendar in its fifth sign, in the Era of — Enkyo 9 (1744-1747) under a sal tree[25].
>
> One who has not yet become a Buddha, so that he may teach others.
>
> A writing by an aged priest.

Letter Written to a Sick Monk Living in a Distant Province

It is very kind of you to have sent news so often in the past by letter and message, and now a revered travelling teacher of the Zen sect has brought a delightful letter from you which seems to enclose, in itself, a peculiar fragrance and freshness of quiet retirement.

For some time, we have been planning to make our 'pilgrim way'[26] to visit you, and we have been waiting to hear some good news that perhaps you have not been obliged by the state of your health to omit your religious duties, and that you have attained to the joy of full fruition. But now we are distressed to hear that since last summer you have been feeling very ill and have been obliged to enter the temple sickroom. However, the report we have had from our revered travelling priest is better, for we hear that your condition is not as serious as we had feared, and that two or three days before he left you, you had been able to enter again into the Main Hall. So we are much happier about you now.

During a serious and long illness many anxieties and other emotions come to us all, but we must leave such feelings and cares to the secular world and determine to set ourselves wholeheartedly to the important duty of preserving the right spirit of meditation. And I have reached the conclusion that one will not fall back or become negligent after a sickness when one preserves that spirit of meditation throughout all the times one has been suffering the pains of illness, even if there be an entire reversal of one's fortune afterwards. So think of your time of sickness as a time of unusual importance, and do not be careless in preserving the right spirit.

Thirty years ago, I who am now an old arhat, wrote a report about sickness and the priesthood. I then pointed out that there is nothing as sad as the sickness of those who only have the wisdom of this world. In proportion to their worldly wisdom they continue to regret in unmeasured terms the times that are past. They find fault with everything, whether good or bad, in those who are caring for them. They feel envious of the good fortune or leisure of their old associates. They are distressed because their fame has not been established during their lifetime and they are fearful about the long night of pain which is to follow their death. When they think of their own native places, they are angry because their wings have not grown. They fret because no favourable response has come from the prayers they have offered to the gods. When they are lying down with closed eyes, they seem to be commendably calm, but inwardly a greater conflict is going on than was the battle of the Nine Countries, and their hearts are full of even greater pain than that of all the sentient beings in the three hell states. A sickness of only three pints is imagined to be one of eight and a half quarts. If they are as crazy as that about their illness when they are dying, one can only guess at the state they will be in after this life!

As we know that quiet thinking and the spirit of meditation is like a medicine for remaining in good health, we would like to visit such persons and lend them our aid so as to enable them to think quietly, but if the very fact of quiet thinking is painful to them, then the fire of their hearts would only flare up the more, the metal of their lungs would only waste away all the more in pain, the moisture of their bodies would dry up, and they would continue to feel cold and hot, and the sweat which steals away the very life itself would become more and more frequent until at last it would be difficult to sustain the roots of life. And all these troubles are due to ordinary everyday carelessness and negligence of will to keep the spirit of meditation. This negligence, together with false illusions, turn what was only a little sickness into a really big illness. So, it is not the sickness which has done the injury, but errors of the heart and mind which devour and kill. In very truth, these errors of the heart and mind are more terrible than any tiger or wolf. Tigers and wolves are not the kind of creatures which come into places enclosed by doors and walls or fences, but these wolves of error of thought climb up onto the floor of meditation and destroy the quiet seat of thought. They are wretches which clothe themselves arbitrarily in the sevenfold and ninefold robes of the priestly dress. There are some sick people who do nothing but weep bitterly and say that there is no one as unlucky as they are. They complain with tremulous voices that it is dreadfully hard to waste away in these bodies of theirs — these bodies which, as they say, only come to them at rare intervals in the cycle of karmic existences. And even in spite of the fact that they may have reached the state of priesthood, they say that they have not been able to heap up merit by their faith in the Way, and have not seen the light of Buddha's Way. Perhaps their complaints might seem sincere and even charming, but their state is only the result of their own negligence and carelessness caused by ignorance.

As a matter of fact, there is really no better occasion than sickness for practising the Way. In ancient times, many wise people concealed themselves in valleys and under cliffs in the deep mountains in order to escape as far as possible from the world. They would keep apart from the secular business of life with the intention of giving themselves wholly to following the Way. But there is no mountain or valley to compare with illness. When one is sick, one does not need to seek out any other mountain or valley. The sick person escapes the tiring toil of alms-collecting, avoids the duties of entertaining visiting priests and others; and is not troubled by the noisy and idle talk of large assemblies. This sick person does not suffer from the disturbing labour of the temple halls and does not feel the anxieties of scarcity recurring after better times in temple life. He can leave the matter of life or death in the hands of heaven. He entrusts the care of his body — whether it is to be kept warm, cold, or fed — to his nurses. He does not have to worry about his body any more than do cats or dogs when they are sick.

The one thing the sick person should not forget when between the quilts of his bed, is to preserve the spirit of meditation. He will remember that life is but a dream, that death too is but a dream. He will give up ideas about heaven, hell, this world or paradise. In the twinkling of an eye, he will turn towards that place where no worldly affairs can trouble him, where he can examine his thoughts about the principles and truth of things. He will persevere in the spirit of meditation as the chief of his tasks. And then he may, almost without knowing it, cross the borders of life and death, transcend the limits of perception and illusion, and come to that state which is called 'the inde-structible, real body of the Diamond Realm'. Is not this, indeed, the discovery of the divine elixir of never growing old and never dying? Is it not the very recollection of one's own birth into this world of humanity? Is it not the dignity attaching to the shaven priesthood? Is it not the spiritual experience of the mystery of the Way of the Buddha?

When a man who comes to the correct method of meditation confronts good luck or bad luck, a good fate or a sad reversal of fortune, all these things become for him the food which strengthens him in the performance of the Way. But in the case of one who is negligent and lazy in this spiritual matter, even quite a trivial occurrence such as sickness no bigger than a mustard seed, becomes an enormous obstacle to that person's progress. Such a result is, in the final analysis, the effect of works done in a prev-ious existence. There is an entire absence of *prajna* (wis-dom). Those sorts of people always give excuses and reasons for drawing away from that real wisdom, which is in fact not really far off. They plant and raise obstacles to the performance of the Way, obstacles which have no real roots. There is nothing as sad and bitter as an error of life like that.

On the other hand, there are many instances of people in ancient times who, though suffering from severe illnesses, broke down all the effects of doubt. There was an old priest, Nagagoro Saru, who suffered from a very bad boil. His back swelled up so much it looked like a bright red winter melon, and the pain he had to endure was almost unbearable. The only thing he could swallow was hot medicine, and he could not let people come near him. He just closed his eyes and lay on his bed in agony.

One day some affectionate friends, associates in the dharma, came to enquire after his health and to comfort him. A surgeon also came that very day to clean the priest's wound and to apply dressings. That night, however, his pain became even worse. It was truly unbelievable that such a material thing as that boil could cause such terrible pain on such a precious body for so many days. When his friends were about to leave — in order to soothe and comfort him — they remarked that it seemed as if his flesh was healing that day, so he would not have long to wait for the delightful and pleasurable feeling of restored health. But the old priest, looking as if he had only just awakened from a deep sleep, said that it was very kind of so many good friends to have come to visit him, and he wanted to confess something. He said he had previously been ashamed to say something, but now he did not wish to conceal it any longer; and he asked them to come close to his bed and listen. Then he said: 'The pains of this sickness have taught me a valuable lesson. By the help of this boil I have learned to see the faults of the past twenty years of my life. Now, at long last, I am feeling the joy of the accomplishment of what has been the true purpose of my life for forty years. Before suffering this boil, I used to think there was nothing lacking in what I believed to be a state of enlightenment, and I thought there was nothing lacking in the religious discipline which I was performing. For that very reason, however, I ceased performing the correct discipline. I was bold enough to accept all kinds of ceremonial honours, and had behaved discourteously towards people. And then suddenly I sank under this severe sickness when all my five limbs began to boil with heat and my joints felt as if they would break to pieces. I sometimes fainted and my mind became closed. I felt the pains of a hell of blackness. The totality of all the hot hell states seemed to be gathered in this little body of mine, and what I had thought to be my enlightenment and vision, disappeared. I could not get even one dram of energy, and nothing was left to me but vain thoughts and pains. Oh, it was dreadful! Certainly no one would have envied me if I were to die in such a state of pain and distress. It did not seem that my life could be saved.

'But then I set myself to meditate correctly, deciding that unless I fought to the limit of my powers, I should never be able to overcome pain nor be victorious in my meditative life. So I exerted myself to burning point, and persevered boldly and courageously; and even though once or twice it became almost too painful to bear, I succeeded in repeating it with that kind of determination over and over again, progressing without ceasing until somehow I won the victory. I permitted no limit of day or night, nor did I allow anything to become an obstacle whether I was lying down or standing up, until at last the spirit of meditation matured in me, as it were, before my very eyes. And now, for the past fourteen or fifteen days I have felt that the illusions and pains of my life have faded away like mist, so that not only is there a great peace in my mind, but I have come to the recognition that life and death, the Buddha and all demons or spirits, are in essence but one. I have, in fact, now penetrated through to the realisation of the mystery of diamond hardness, that the dharmas or elements of existence are, in reality, of one essence. From this very day I know that, no matter what reversals of fortune may befall me, there is nothing which can be an obstacle to my enlightenment. Oh, that many others might also seek for understanding and attain to some of the energy which will wake them up so that they too might rise up as did I, this foolish old man that I am! I repeat again that when one is healthy, one must not be negligent about the meditative life. This sickness of mine has been a gracious sickness, and there is nothing for which I am more thankful. The more I think about it, the more it seems to me that this boil has been of unsurpassed benefit in providing me with true wisdom. And now, when I ponder over the sort of spiritual duty which I ought to perform and the amount of praise I should offer, I almost regret that this boil is being cured!' The old priest concluded with a bright smile. That is what we have been told by the friends who were attending him at the time.

Or, again, there was that hermit — revered as one of the teachers of the Shingon sect — who was taken ill with a severe attack of typhoid fever. His groans did not cease by day or night, and his young attendants impertinently re-marked: 'This is not at all like the old man's true dispo-sition. And the noise he makes does not sound like the scoldings he gives us — just listen to that moaning and groaning!' And they laughed at him. But the old hermit laughed too, and said: 'Hello there, you young fellows! The groaning you have been listening to for several days was just the noise caused by my disease, but now, today, it has changed. It has become the sound of a great mystery. If you laugh at me now in mockery, you may receive the punishment due to those who mock the dharma.' The young acolytes immediately changed their attitude and said that the old hermit had become a veritable god, that he had suddenly and quickly reached buddhahood — as quickly as a man can turn over his hand. The old hermit continued: 'The Buddha passed through the three ages[27] to nirvana for the sake of sentient beings who are negligent in their meditative life. And for the sake of others who are bold and courageous in that life, he taught that buddhahood can be reached in an instant, in a flash. I myself indeed suffered pains which were hard to bear, and my suffering was from things which have no reality in their nature. I spent my time in fear of the pains merited by me which might come to me in the coming life. Also, I wept in repentance of the works done in my previous life, but now my thoughts have changed. I have entered into the perception of the uniqueness of Vairocana. I closed my eyes, gritted my teeth, and immediately found that I had begun to progress in diligence; and how wonderful it is! All the pains of my sickness have melted away. This old body of mine which had been lying so sick, has been revealed to me as the very *dharani*[28] (treasure seal) of the yoga mystery! All unknown to me, the true body of the diamond hardness has been brought to maturity in me. So the voices of my groans have changed, and they are now united with and mixed with the great "*dharanis* of the three mysteries".[29] The bed on which I lie is now the great mandala throne of Vairocana's true nature. The fourfold rounded altar of the mandala now shines out brightly before the eyes of my mind. Oh, how happy I am! All things which exist and possess the buddha-nature, and all things which exist apart from that nature, have now been perfected in the Way; they have reached the goal of the Way. Herbs, trees, the very earth itself, have brought to fulfilment their primary and original desire to attain to buddhahood.'

His attendants did not, of course, understand what the old priest had told them merely by hearing his words, but they congratulated themselves on having been in the company of such bright sunshine shed forth by buddha-compassion. They could not refrain from reporting what they had heard and seen, and they did so with tears of joy. Never was there greater activity in the Way!

In foreign lands too, there were people like Toyaku of Shuko, and Rishitsu of Mount Ko, and others who made progress in the Heart-Way of the Buddha through sickness. Unfortunately, the priests of our land and of this age have not benefited by sickness and, oh dear, there does seem to be a lack of lustre amongst them! Why is it, I wonder, that we are so much worse than the men of old?

Even if death is not imminent, a man will be a true descendant of the patriarchs if, at the time of his death, he has performed joyfully the discipline of spiritual meditation. When I say this, of course, I hope you will not think I am advising people to wait for a serious sickness before starting the meditative life. Everybody who, in spite of not being in good health like those I have mentioned, who has bravely and continuously attended to this matter — everyone, I say, ten out of ten, a hundred out of a hundred — will bring the Way to maturity. At any rate, it is clear that there is nothing so precious and important as the meditative life. Let those who have not straightforwardly entered enlightenment, go to a reliable guide and begin this decisive work from the start. After the first decisive step has been taken, the chief thing to remember is never to cease from the spirit of meditation in whichever of the four postures one rests. As the sage, Daie Zenshi, said: 'One can never know whether one may lose the opportunity, or when one may find it. Therefore, wherever one may be, one must carry on with one's practice.' And all the sages who followed him showed this sort of carefulness in their performance of the meditative life. This is, in truth, the correct, ancient and unchangeable form of the meditative practice. It is known as 'the true heart', 'buddha-nature', 'bodhi', 'nirvana', or 'the true constant man'. The 'true man' of this nature has never throughout the ages, or in this latter age of 'destruction', any sensation of sickness, nor even will the colour of his nose change! In the *Sutra of the Lotus*, the man of this nature is highly praised as being the manifestation in bodily form of the most ancient Buddha, the Buddha who was the first to be manifested in all the cycles of the ages.

In the Patriarch Nangaku's book, *On the Forty-Sixth Vow of Amitabha Buddha (The Zui-I Gan Gyo)*, these words occur: 'What was called the Lotus Law on the Vulture Peak is now in the western land called Amitabha. In the last times it will be called Avalokiteshvara (Kannon).' He is really speaking of this 'true man'. This 'true man' must be served with reverence, and approached with courtesy. If one comes near to him with a friendly feeling, there is no sickness which cannot be cured; there is no Way which cannot be accomplished. Even an emaciated old man or a sick old woman, may become a healthy, energetic person provided he or she perseveres in preserving the spirit of meditation in the Buddha Way. On the other hand, even if one has a body seven or eight feet tall and wisdom corresponding to its height, even if one has a rich supply of benevolence to explain the teaching, even if one is able to lecture on the Three Sutras[30] and the Five Sacred Books,[31] even if one has studied thoroughly the secret teachings of the Five Schools of Thought and the Seven Sects,[32] even if one has the full amount of required energy, and even if one's eyes can penetrate the universe — unless one possesses the uninterrupted spirit of meditation, such a one is nothing but a corrupting corpse. No one should take an easy posture and decide that this possession of the spirit of meditation is an easy matter, for it is truly hard to preserve and to persevere in this life.

The saddest thing about this last kalpa or age of ours is that people are set on making their own names famous.

The heart for obtaining wealth is flourishing. Many people make a show of possessing the heart which is searching for the Way, as if that were a sort of ornament to exhibit. Yet it is hard to find anyone who has truly made up his or her mind to carry on the spirit of meditation. And it is still harder to find anyone who possesses the spirit continuously. There is not one in a thousand, no, not one in ten thousand!

I myself came to see this when I was thirteen years old. When I was sixteen I broke away from the sexual life. When I was nineteen I left the world. When I was thirty-five I came to live at this temple. Now sixty-five years have elapsed. During the forty years of my middle age, all worldly affairs were given up and all secular avocations were omitted. I guarded myself with sincere application and now for the past five or six years, I have been able to stay with the spirit of meditation without intermission. If, however, a man fawns on his temple patrons and alms-paying parishioners in a light-hearted way, or if he is always hoping for benefits or some support or fame whilst trying to perform his meditation, that is just like having a great pain in one's insides. More often than not these days, teachers and pupils live together in temples making luxury and opulence the object of their lives. The atmosphere of the temple is one of heated busy crowds. People think that the gift of the gab and being smart, are signs of wisdom. Their food is exquisite and their dress is superfine. The Buddhist world is now filled with people of their sort. They have come to think that virtue consists only in the admiration of great and beautiful things, and that if a man merely believes the forms of faith, he has reached perfection in the attainment of dharma. It is lamentable that they make use of their bodies merely to get fame for themselves

— these bodies which are so hard to come by in the course of the cycles of existence — and they bury the buddha-heart under the rubbish heap of illusions. They adorn themselves unstintingly with silks and damasks which do not harmonise with ceremonies or rituals anywhere. They scatter expositions of the *dhyana* teaching and the Buddhadharma without understanding it themselves. And with regard to their treatment of the white-robed laity, what Komei Shibo said so eloquently is quite true: 'They have the magic powers of a Maudgalyayana in getting hold of or stealing the alms of the laity which the laity have produced by the sweat of their brows.' They deliberately forget their beliefs in the law of karma when they want to obtain some short-lived benefit for themselves. They relieve themselves of any fear of due recompense, but there is no mistake as to what will eventually happen to them. The last day of the winter solstice of their lives will come upon them when but one solitary light is left burning. Then they will weep and wail on the verge of death. They will suffer the 'seven upsets' of faith and be filled with the panic fears of hellish states. They will wriggle and flounder about as they die, without having any place to put their heads or feet, and they will lie with their faces to the ground even in the presence of their disciples.

But when one remembers the disposition of the people of our times, is there anybody in any of our provinces who might not become a Buddhist patriarch if that person sincerely practised the rule of the meditative life? I ask myself why I should teach these hard things to people who come to me at a dismal place like this to go into retreat? Here I live in a tumble-down old house, quite separated from the world, where there is no easy-going heart-calming Buddhadharma for me. But there is nothing worse, I think, than a religious monk who is proud and treats his own body delicately.

One year, when a large pack of wolves roamed around this village at the foot of these hills, one old fool of a priest went and spent seven nights sitting in one or other of the graveyards. He did this so that he might test himself. He wanted to see whether he could retain the spirit of meditation without interruption even whilst the wolves sniffed round his ears and breathed down his neck. When any creature, even a naiad or a serpent, has made up its mind boldly to perform any duty, is it right for that creature to leave the duty unfinished? Surely, that creature must not let the duty remain unaccomplished. He should endure any amount of cold or hunger, suffer any amount of rain and storm, go to the bottom of pits of fire or dive under ice, so as to keep open and awake the eyes which the Buddha has opened, and so that he may reach the fields the Buddha has reached, so that he may carry on the great work of religious teaching to the bitter end, until he penetrates through to the final mystery. He must admonish the priests of all the ten regions of the universe, draw out the nails, undo the lynch-pins of falsehood, and show his gratitude for the overflowing measure of Buddha's compassion.

If anyone is zealous enough in performing the great Buddha Vow to the degree necessary for the cycle of existence to cease, every sort of sickness will be crowded out of that person's life. But it must never be forgotten that everybody who has virtuously practised this discipline without negligence has experienced something of the bitter hardness of wearing the black robes, of the first steps of discipleship, of pity, and of the light. But if one becomes negligent, then one will become a devotee in outward show only. And when I say outward show, what I mean is that it will be a sham. Though there is no one who wishes to be a sham, especially if one has no lack of physical necessities, yet such people may easily become obvious examples of shams if they do not seek and accept the advice of good friends, and do not seek the Way from the depths of their hearts, but rely on their own superficial understanding and talk a great deal about it just for the sake of making themselves admired by their friends. So, be careful in what you do, persevere in carrying on the spirit of meditation, and then if things do not seem sufficient for you, you may go and starve yourself or freeze yourself to death in some distant valley or on some mountain. 'Gold wrapped in straw remains gold.' Let the avatar deities place their hands together and pay their respects. Let the dragon deities bow their heads and give protection to one who is a true descendant of the Buddha. On the other hand, if one has piled up treasures by flattery and obsequiousness, and if that person's funeral is attended by a thousand priests, and the ceremonies are those of the seven treasures,[33] and men's eyes are entranced by the brilliant funeral banners, and the mind is astonished by the gorgeousness of the mandala seat — yet if the eyes of Enma, the king of hell, are flashing with anger and the ox-headed demons are waiting with their whips, twisting and twirling them — that will be a bitter, bitter thing.

What I have told you is what was related by the old priest, Shoju, to two or three attendant priests. They listened to him from the first part of the hour of the Dog (8.00 pm) until the third part of the hour of the Ox (3.00 am), and it seemed to them as though it were but an instant of time. So deeply impressed were they by what he told them, that tears of gratitude ran down their faces. At the same time, however, their bodies became wet with the perspiration of shame. After hearing this statement of the old priest, I would recall it whenever I suffered from any kind of sickness, and I too could never help but feel shame for my own imperfections, after which my pains seemed to get less. So I hope that by sending you just an outline of that old priest's statement, my letter may be of some little help to you in your ills, and also to those who are attending you in the sickroom of your temple. It was this sort of medicine that the old priest, Shoju, used to dispense as his normal treatment, just one ingredient in his 'cold shock regulating' method of cures.

And here I will add another method which is especially good for weak people. It is a marvellous method of saving people from weariness of spirit. It allays the rush of blood to the head; it warms the limbs; it soothes the bowels; it improves the eyesight; it increases wisdom and it is especially efficacious for ridding the mind of false knowledge. The medicine is compounded in the following way. Take one grain of soft cream of the elixir pill, one slice of 'recognition of the real aspects of all dharmas or elements of existence', one drop each of 'knowledge that both the self and dharmas are void', three drops of 'knowledge of how immediate entry to nirvana is obtained', two drops of 'no lusts or desires', three drops of 'realisation that the life of activity and the life of quiet are not two separate things'. Add one-and-a-half of the minutest quantities of the skin of the sponge gourd, and one slice of 'ridding oneself of all attachment to things'. Soak all the above ingredients for a whole night in patience, and pound it up in a dry, shady spot. Discipline oneself according to the precedents set for one in the *Prajnaparamita sutras*. Make all this up into a ball the size of a duck's egg and place it restfully on the top of your head.'

But whoever undertakes this cure must not begin by asking such questions as: 'What sort of medicine is this?' or 'How heavy is it?' All one has to do is to remember that an egg-sized pill with a delicious scent, feeling like cream, is resting on top of one's head. When the sick person needs to use this medicine he should place a thick cushion beneath him for his seat, straighten his back, close his eyes and sit in an upright posture. Then move his body gently backwards and forwards and settle down to his meditation. There is nothing to compare with this method of cure for prolonging life and nourishing the spirit. When the spirit is exhausted then the body dies, just as when the people deteriorate, the state will perish.

Think over this whole matter three times. Repeat the sensation which will come to you. There will be a wonderful sensation throughout your whole body when you have that medicine placed on your head, a medicine like a duck's egg made of cream. Your head will begin to feel damp. Then the whole body will begin to feel damp from the shoulders to the elbows, both breasts, the diaphragm, the lungs, the liver, the stomach, the back down to the buttocks. Next, all the constrictions in the chest, all the pains of the body, constipation, indigestion, all of these troubles will be calmed down in company with the mind — as surely as water seeks the low levels. One's voice will become clear, and one's whole body will become filled, as it were, with flowing water until even one's legs become warm right down to the soles of the feet. This sensation should be repeated by the person who is practising meditation. The overflowing of this penetrating moisture saturates and steeps the body in warmth. It can be compared with a medicine which a good secular physician might prescribe when he has collected various herbs, brewed them, filled up his bowls with the mixture, and then bandages them on our bodies below the navel.

Whilst experiencing this sensation, provided one preserves the thought in one's mind that all objects of sense are but ideas in the mind, then one will begin to notice a delicious and rare odour. There will come a feeling of softness of touch to the skin. One's body and mind will become entirely harmonised and in accord with each other. Immediately, all the elements *(skandhas)* of existence are dissolved. Also, one's internal organs become calm and quiet. A lustre shines on the skin, and the bodily energy is greatly increased.

If one repeats this sensation from time to time in its completeness, there will be no sickness which cannot be healed; there will be no mystic act which cannot be performed. For this is indeed the mystic secret of prolonging life, the mystic art of immortality. This treatment originated with Konsen Shi, and later was handed down to Chisha Daishi. He was cured of a severe disease by it. It also saved the life of his elder brother, Chui Shin. It is the mystical treatment handed down to us from the final age of the era of Gyo. But seldom do men of our times attain to the knowledge of this Way.

I myself heard of it in my middle life from Hakuyu who told me that its efficacy and the speed with which it takes effect, depends upon the zeal or lack of zeal in carrying it out. If one is zealous and not negligent in practising it, one will attain a long life. And, now, please do not say: 'Oh, old Hakuin is expounding a method of meditation for old women.' Try it, and you may obtain knowledge of the Buddha voice. Then you will be able to clap your hands and laugh with glee.

As has been well said: 'Until one has experienced the disorders of a rebellion, one does not see the virtue of the honest minister of state. Until one has come into the possession of wealth, one does not know what the will of a righteous man is.'

Self-portrait by
Hakuin Zenji

**By courtesy of the
Abbot of Shoin
Temple, Shizuoka-
ken.**

Reply to an Aged Nun of the Hokke Sect

It seems you have read a resumé of some of my lectures on the *Lotus Sutra* delivered last autumn. In them I said that 'outside of the mind there is no *Lotus Sutra*, and outside the *Lotus Sutra* there is no mind'. You tell me that you think this a strange idea, and you ask me to explain by letter the meaning of my statements. You also say that you would like me to add any other suggestions which I think might be helpful in elucidating the subject. So here I will give the main purport of the lectures, and hope you will not mind reading it several times in order to get the ideas thoroughly into your mind.

Yes, it is true, as we have always taught, that outside or apart from the mind there is no *Lotus Sutra*, and outside or apart from the *Lotus Sutra* there is no mind. Outside the mind there are not ten worlds of illusion and enlightenment.[34] Nor is there any *Lotus Sutra* outside these ten realms. This is indeed the highest point of reasoning attained by meditative thought. And it is not I alone, but all the *tathagatas* of the three ages (past, present and future) as well as the scholars and sages of the ten regions of the universe, who, at the final stage of their teaching, explain the matter in this way. All of them have said that the substance of the teaching of the *Lotus Sutra* is directed to establishing this great truth. Of course, it is the case that besides this essential teaching of the *Lotus Sutra*, there have been promulgated the 'eighty-four thousand schools' of the dharma of the Buddha. These are all considered to be concerned with accommodated truth. None of them can be excluded from that sphere of accommodated truth.

The final teaching, however, is that reality can only be explained as being of one nature only. All sentient beings, the *tathagatas* of the three ages and ten regions, all mountains, rivers, this great earth, and the very *Lotus Law* itself are not of two distinct natures. They are identical — that is to say, of one nature. All aspects of the universe — the relative and the absolute — are but one in reality. Such is a brief summary of the teaching of the Buddha's Way.

As a matter of history, in the time of the first World Revered One, there was the 'quick' teaching or the 'sudden' teaching, the 'gradual' and the secret or 'mystic' teachings.[35] By use of these various forms of teaching, the World Revered One taught that, though there were 5,408 volumes of scripture, the ultimate purport of them all might be found contained within one section of the eight volumes of the *Lotus Sutra*. And still further, the ultimate purport of that law of the *Lotus Sutra*, with its more than 4,360 ideograms, might be found contained within the five ideograms: *Myo-Ho-Ren-Ge-Kyo* (Wondrous-Law-Lotus-Blossom-Sutra). And the meaning of these five ideograms is contained in the two words: *'Myo Ho'* or 'Wondrous Law'. And in the final analysis these two words are, in effect, contained in the one great word: 'Mind'.

Now, if you want to know what this great word 'mind' leads us to, think of that ancient poem which runs: 'The tortoise crosses the hills of separation — and what does it reach at the end? If you wish to know what it is which spoils the eternal purpose of springtime, stop using your needle and keep silence — then you will know.'

Consider this word 'one-mind', which is the Wondrous Law. When looked at from the aspect of extension or outwardly, it embraces the ten regions of the universe. When looked at from the aspect of intensity or inwardly, it is reduced to an essence of non-thought or non-mind. It was this which the World Revered One meant when he taught that outside mind there are no elements *(dharmas)* of existence, and that the three worlds, the whole of existence, exist in the mind alone, and that all aspects of reality are but One. And so the conclusion of his teaching is that the ultimate truth is called 'the Law of the Lotus Blossom, and the eternal Buddha'. In Zen it is known as the 'original dignity of the person'. In Shingon it is known as the 'sun's disc of fundamental non-birth'. In the Ritsu teaching it is known as the 'essence of dharma-nature'.

Please remember that all these are but different names for the one mind. But perhaps you will ask: 'What evidence is there for the statement that the five ideograms *"myo-ho-ren-ge-kyo"* signify the source of the one mind?' I reply that surely the very words themselves provide sufficient evidence. The words are the title of the book which sings the praises of the merit and power of the mystery of the mind. They are a phrase pointing to and illustrating the marvellous nature of this one mind.

Think first of some lesser matters which will illustrate this point. Think of the work which one does with one's hands — painting pictures and such arts. We say that so-and-so has the wondrous art of playing the biwa or koto. But if you proceed to ask where that wondrous art resides, not even the greatest orator can find words to give a good answer. A father is not able to teach his beloved child by words those arts which come down from father to son. When it is this wondrous art, it is something which is produced by an operation unknown to us. This is the mind-nature operating as the wondrous law in people's daily activities.

You will perhaps laugh at or argue about this letter, but, all the same, is it not a remarkable thing that out of every five or ten persons you meet, every one of them continues to perform his or her own function without error — just like a ring which goes on spinning out its thread endlessly? And if you ask what it is which goes on functioning automatically and endlessly and freely like this, then look inwards and you will find that it is nothing that you can discover by smelling or hearing. It is something entirely empty, neutral and without marks. If you make a guess that it is like wood or stone, you will find that it is something which changes a thousand times, which has a thousand different appearances and which is free and independent. If you say that it has sentient existence, you will find that that is not the case. Again, if you say that it has no sentient existence, you will find that it is a non-existent entity! So, because words fail to express it, the Revered One gave this 'transcendent thing' the provisional name 'Wondrous Law'.

And then there is the word 'scripture' or 'sutra'. The ideogram means or points to the idea of permanence, and the Revered One used it to signify the permanence of buddha-nature. So the Revered One used this word *'kyo'* *(sutra)* with reference to the permanency of buddha-nature. The mind-nature is not increased when it exists in the Buddha, nor is it diminished when it exists within sentient beings. It comes from the same originating impulse as heaven and earth; it is of the same 'substance' as the universe; it has not altered in the least since before the ages began, nor will it alter in the least after the ages end. So when the Revered One extolled the wondrous law as being the essence of buddha-mind, and when he called that wondrous law of the buddha-mind the *Lotus Blossom Sutra*, he was merely using different names for one and the same thing: the one mind. One reality, two names. Just as the name *'mochi'* signifies the same thing as *'o-kachin'* (rice cake).

Now, if this real, essential, *Lotus Law Sutra* is something which cannot be touched with the hands nor seen with the eyes, how does one get hold of it? What sort of preparation is needed for a person to become a practitioner of this *Lotus Sutra*? Well, there are three kinds. There is the lower grade activating impulse which makes one take hold of the golden scroll and its red lacquered holder and just read, intone, copy or expound it. There is the medium grade activating impulse which makes one get hold of it by illuminating or reflecting on it in one's own mind. Then there is the upper grade activating impulse to read the Sutra with the eyes, penetrate through to its depths, and see it as if it were one's own face. This is what is meant in the *Mahaparinirvana Sutra (Nehan-kyo)* where it says: 'The Tathagata sees the buddha-nature with his own eyes.'

The practice of this Lotus Law is the ultimate end of the devotional discipline of the Mahayana teaching, and it is by no means an easy matter. What is easy is very easy, but what is hard is very hard. In the text of the sutra itself it says: 'This sutra is hard to hold, but if one holds it for a short time one immediately feels joy.' This is what all the buddhas have taught. And it is of supreme importance to practise it. Chisha, the founder of the Tendai School in China, said: 'Even without taking this scroll into your hands, read it all the time. Without repeating the words with your mouth, intone this whole ritual wherever you happen to be. The Buddha, without expounding the dharma, is always hearing the sound of the dharma. Without bringing thoughts into his mind, he is all the time enlightening the whole universe.' That is the only correct method of reciting this sutra.

And then one asks tentatively: 'What sort of sutra is this, then, which one recites without holding it in one's hands?' Is it not the wondrous law of one's own mind? And those words: 'Without raising thoughts in one's mind, one illuminates the whole universe.' What do they signify? Surely, they signify the real, essential lotus blossom. It is what we call 'the sutra without words'. People who take the golden scroll and its handle into their hands and think that they have taken hold of the Lotus Law, are like sick people who lick the paper on which the medical prescription is written, and think that that will cure their illness! Such people are in a sad way. If you wish to hold on to this sutra throughout the twelve hours of the day and night, without a single speck of cloudiness or any break within you, then you will have to discipline yourself in the merit-bringing work of non-thinking of good, and non-thinking of evil. This is the correct method.

With regard to this, the sage Jittoku said in one of his *gathas*: 'If you wish to know what is meant by the "non-originated,"[36] do not let any threads hang in your mind.' This sums up the correct meditative discipline from which all the *tathagatas* of the three ages started, as well as all the wise ones and all the great priests; and it is the method by which they attained the great enlightenment. It is the sum of their ancient and unchanging teaching. It is a matter of instantaneous non-birth, of the cutting off of before and after, so it is not unreasonable that the Tathagata should have told us that it is hard to hold on to this sutra, for it is the direct road to quick enlightenment and the attainment of buddhahood. Practically all the sages and teachers are of the same opinion about this when they speak of the ultimate truth. They may perhaps have differed as to the depth and fineness of their own efforts to progress in the discipline, and in the height to which they attained, but the direction of their steps has always been the same.

Each school gives a different name to this ultimate goal. In the Confucian teaching it is called the 'Highest Good' or the 'Unoriginated Mean'. The Taoists call it the 'Void of Non-Nature'. Shintoists call it 'Takamagahara' (the Shinto land of the gods). In the Tendai teaching it is the 'Great Instantaneous *Shamatha* or Cessation of the Three Thousand Mental Activities'. In the Shingon doctrine it is called 'The Dharma of the Perception of the Non-Birth of the Adi Buddha'. When the patriarchs of all these families of doctrine urge us to go to meditation or to read the sutras, to read and re-read, to recite and re-recite, and to do so with a single mind and undisturbed heart, so that we may at last reach the fields of pure non-confusion, they are teaching the truth accommodated to our conditions, are they not?

Dogen, the founder of Eihei-ji, said: 'One day on which this duty is performed is much to be valued. One hundred years in which it is not performed are a hundred years much to be regretted.' Truly, one cannot but shed tears of sorrow for those who live in the distressful and shallow sense-world where they possess human bodies which are so hard to come by in the long cycle of the existences of karma ages, and yet never practise any meditation throughout all their human lives. They rot away without any understanding, and are surely on their way back to those three regions of hell which they are so afraid of. What is hard is very hard indeed!

But it also says that 'what is easy is very easy'. What then does that mean? I would reply to my questioner by asking him just to put out his hand to the sutra and quietly hold on to the practice of meditation, and make up his mind to look just once at the true dignified beauty of the law blossom. If only once a person catches a glimpse of the true dignity of the law blossom, then everything — every action (even coughing, writing, sitting, talking, working) and every shrub, tree, tile, stone, sentient being and non-sentient being — every one of them will instantly become as perfect as the *Wondrous Law of the Lotus Blossom Sutra*. They will all and every one appear as in true harmony with this sutra. Why then should anybody want to hold on to any other method?

If anyone thinks that he can estimate the value of the Lotus Blossom Law without glancing at the real lotus blossom, he may be compared to a man who holds up a cup of water in his hand, determined to keep it day and night without spilling or moving it, and prays that he may thus increase the sustenance for his body. Even if he succeeded in holding it up throughout his life, it is obvious that he would not thereby sustain himself, nor be able to satisfy his thirst or that of his family. He would soon lose all hope of carrying out such vows as those of the two benefits, i.e. to save himself by his own efforts and to save others. Of what use would long perseverance in holding up the cup have been? But if one fixes one's gaze on the real essential lotus blossom and holds on to *this* sutra, that person might be compared to one who poured that cup of water into the rivers and lakes of the world. Immediately, thirty-six thousand sparkling little waves would be formed, and the good quality of the water poured in would act together with the great waters, and would help to nourish all creatures which fly, run, and crawl, for they could come to drink at those waters without limit. He who does not look at the lotus blossom, is like one who holds up a cup of water. Not only does he not provide any benefit for others, he cannot even provide benefit for himself. He who looks at the real essential lotus blossom, is like one who pours the cup of water into the great waters of the stream of this world's life. All unknowingly, he pours it into the ocean of the great calm of all the buddhas. There it is harmoniously united with the wisdom of the true *dharmakaya* (dharma-body) of the Buddha. And at the same time it breaks to pieces the dark cave of the eighth consciousness, and sends forth the bright light of the great mirror[37] of absolute wisdom, so that all the chief practices of the dharma are exhaustively fulfilled during the ages of delusion. One of the main merits of looking at the real essential lotus blossom is that in it there is no upper or lower, there are no four directions to face, nor are there any classes or parts in it.

It is better for people to set their gaze on the law blossom than to study all the other sutras, no matter how earnestly. It is better for people to set their gaze on the real law blossom than to build stupas to contain inexhaustible treasures. It is better for people to set their gaze on the real law blossom than to set up a million images of the Buddha. It is better for people to set their gaze on the real law blossom than to study all the mysteries of the three worlds. It is better to set one's gaze on the real law blossom than to take up the golden scroll with its red-lacquered handle and to become attached to that outward sutra. It is better to set one's gaze on the real lotus blossom than to intone the *Lotus Sutra* a million times. Such is, indeed, the highest counsel of those who are accomplished practitioners of the dharma.

And what is the method by which we may penetrate through to see the real, essential dignity and beauty of the law blossom? Well, we have learned that the wondrous law of the original existent being is the one-mind — so there is nothing better for our purpose than our own mind. Make one's own mind the object in which to look for the law blossom. And what is this mind of ours which we wish to look at? Is it something white or red? Try every possible means to understand this matter. Be bold and resolute in your determination to consider this matter. Make a vow to study it day and night. Of course, there are many methods of coming to this study of the mind, but amongst them all, there is none which surpasses the method of practising the law blossom *samadhi*.

Now, concerning this law blossom *samadhi*, from the very instant you make up your mind to practise it, repeat the great formula, and carry on repeating it without cessation, in grief or sorrow, in hardship or happiness, whether sitting down or standing up, whether asleep or awake, continually repeat the formula: *namu myo ho renge kyo (Hail Wondrous Law of the Lotus Sutra)*. Make this your 'pilgrim staff', your strength to rely on, and with the deep wish to see through to the real dignity and beauty of the law blossom. Continue repeating it. It is well to make each intake of breath and each expiration into a repetition of the formula carefully and ceaselessly repeating it. If you are careful to remain concentrated on this phrase, before long you will find that the mind-nature has become settled in you like a great rock — immoveable and peaceful — and your sensations will not be unrelated to those felt when one dwells on Mount Sumeru. But do not then leave off, rather be even more concentrated and incessant.

Then what one often hears about will take place and the proper spirit of meditation will come upon you. Your usual, everyday consciousness will cease, and it will be as though you have entered the Diamond Sphere, as though you are seated upon the Emerald Throne. You will have one discursive thought, and all of a sudden you will find you are no different from one who has reached the depth of death. Then you may renew your breathing, and quite unconsciously the one, pure, clear truth, all in one whole, will rise up before your very eyes, and you will instantly attain to the true dignified beauty of the lotus blossom. Then the Tathagata, the primeval and eternal reality, will appear before you, and nothing will be able to make him depart from you — even if you try to push him away! This is when you enter what is called in the Tendai School, 'the calm of the absolute, and the treasure house of calm and perpetual light'. This is when you will be enlightened by what the Shingon sect calls, 'The sunlight of the non-origin of the Adi Buddha'. This is when you accomplish what the Jodo (Pure Land) sect calls, 'The fundamental purpose of immediate heart-birth into the Pure Land'. Now you will see before your own eyes the sublime wonders of the Buddha, the Dharma, and the Sangha — all the beautiful waterbirds in the trees of the forest. Now your eyes will be opened to see the truth that this universe and the absolute are identical. Now there can be no doubt that you will reach those fields of Amitabha's third vow, where trees, shrubs and the whole earth are gold with the attainment of buddhahood. So, what is there in this world or in the land of the gods which can be compared with this? It was for this that the buddhas of the three ages left the world for the religious life.

With regard to the efficacy of the sacred formula, there
is no difference between one repetition of the phrase and
the use of one model subject for meditation which we use
in the Zen system. And an old priest like myself would not
write this sort of thing if I thought I might be endangering
my grey hairs by committing the sin of saying what I did
not believe to be true. I have written lengthily and it might
seem unnecessarily, for there are the sages and holy men
of the three ages and ten regions of the universe and more
than eighty thousand deities in the land of the Rising Sun
— all of whom will bear witness to the truth of what I have
said. So do not have any doubt about this matter. Carry on
without becoming negligent, and that feeling which in Zen
manner we call 'grasping the left hand and biting the
middle finger', will grow stronger and stronger.

These days it is often said that it is useless to go to meditation because when you have finished pondering over the
model subject (koan), what will happen? If, they continue,
one knows the heart of the Buddha by sudden intuition,
then why should one grieve if thoughts do arise in one's
mind, or be glad when thoughts cease to arise. Is not White
Tree (the bandit of the mountains) better off just with his
own innate being? When they say, that unless lacquer is
painted on, there will be no surface to peel off, it is as foolish as a blind turtle crawling into an empty hole and then
quitting it, and being satisfied with that sort of thing. What
such people say is only the heretical outer teaching of
some of the nature sects of India. If anybody were to con-
fuse such teaching with the teaching of the sublime heart
of Buddha, even the country bumpkins living at the back
of the village would clench their fists and roar with
laughter. People who say such foolish things are those who
'recognise' the real existence of a soul. It is people like that

who are criticised in the *Shurangama Sutra* where they are said to 'recognise' known bandits as their own children. They do not perceive the reality of the primary pure light. In particular, they do not know about the Tathagata; they do not know that though he had completely destroyed in himself all the delusions spoken of by those holy men who had come to the four final results, though he had reached the truth about the dharma of the self, and was indeed supplied with mystic powers so that his fame had spread throughout the world, yet, even so, he would not allow that to be called 'the attainment of *dhyana*'.

So too it is said in the sutras: 'Even the great arhats cannot expound the meaning of this. It is only the great bodhisattvas who can do so.' And some people who have not even the merit of discriminating insight, dare to call themselves 'venerable persons'! What sort of mind is that?

To sum up, there is nothing which surpasses repeating the sacred formula, providing all attachment to things is cut off. But one must not be one-sidedly attached to the merit of repeating the sacred formula. Do not think that the Shingon or Jodo teachings are worse or lower! People who belong to the Jodo sect by merit of calling whole-heartedly upon the sacred name (of Amida), are quite assured that they will at some time see the Pure Land of the one and only mind and the wonderful form of Amida Buddha. And so they ceaselessly carry on repeating their sacred phrase — as earnestly as if they were trying to save their hair from catching fire! They realise that the Buddha is not far from them. How could it be that such people should not have the vision of the 'tree of the seven treasures' and the 'lake of the eight virtues'? And people who belong to the Shingon sect too; they have the sublime power of their marvellous mystic symbols, their *dharanis*. They have assurance in their praise of the great sun's disc, and the mystic symbol of the Adi Buddha — just as do those who promote the meditative spirit by concentrating on the model subjects (koan) of Zen. When people of that sect continuously rouse themselves to persevere in their practice — Kobo Daishi (774-835), founder of the Shingon sect in Japan, assured them they would no more revolve round the cycle of existence — then how is it possible that they should fail to polish and make perfect their true unbreakable Diamond Body?

And again, it is extremely foolish to think that one must wait until after one's death before obtaining all these benefits. It is also the most culpable negligence. Do not grieve as though this is all a matter of something in the far distance. If it was a matter of having to see or hear something in China or India far beyond the sevenfold tides of the seas, one might grieve. But what we are trying to do, is to look at our own mind with our own mind — and that is something closer to us than looking at the pupils of our eyes with our eyes. And do not grieve as if it were something very deep that we are trying to look at. If it were a matter of something to be seen or listened to at the bottom of the ninefold chasm or under the thousand-fathomed depths of the sea, we might grieve, but to look at my own heart with my own heart, is less than smelling my own nose with my own nostrils!

This age may be the final age, but the dharma is not the last age. To say that this is the final age, and therefore to reject the dharma and pay no respect to it, may be compared to starving and freezing oneself whilst entering the treasure mountain itself! And even if this is the last age, do not be afraid! Fulfil the purpose of your life. Think of the chief priest of the Eshin-in temple in the province of Omi, or still nearer to you, the resident priest of Akazawa or Engu in the Yamashiro province. All of these men fulfilled the purpose of their lives by virtue of calling upon the name. Honen Shonin (1133-1212) founder of the Jodo (Pure Land) sect in Japan, held this wish strongly, but because he had no one to lead him at the time, he said he felt that his wings were too short and that he could not fly in the midheavens!

There *are* signs that this is the final age and the end of the dharma age. Evil customs have arisen. Priests and householders are making themselves believe that any plan to realise the buddha-mind of the wondrous law in these days is comparable to the efforts of an eel trying to climb a tree. What a shallow idea! They are just passing through life in darkness.

Suppose, for example, a farmer has many children and he intends distributing his surplus land amongst them. One of his sons is weak, incapable, talkative and impertinent. This young one says: 'Nowadays it is unreasonable for poor fellows like us to have to learn the customs and ways of our ancestors, to work at farming and bringing up large families. Why, a duck might as well try to imitate a hawk, or join up with a stork and mend its wings when it is on the point of falling, or like a lame tortoise trying to imitate a carp by straining out its neck in an attempt to climb up a waterfall. It is altogether too ridiculous! To go on like that would be nothing but a trick, like trying to drink water off a sickle! I can't understand it at all. People like ourselves, of the lower virtues, are no better than tired children. We cut, we mow, we cultivate fields where weeds are as thick as jungle grass, we pour water over the fields, we plough, we sow seeds, we transplant seedlings, we plant little trees, we reap, we winnow, we grind ears of corn, we twist rope,

we weave matting, we sit with our legs crossed and stare
into nothingness. We live the ordinary humdrum life of
farming peasants. It is all nothing but an old, old story.
Everything seems to be set up in the wrong way. There
ought to be some way in which we could pass through this
life peacefully without having to put our arms through the
sleeves of working clothes. One would like to spend three
or five days travelling to places one hears about where
there is no such thing as having a back without anything to
wear on it, or a mouth without anything to put into it. And
especially, we would like to go to such places as those in
somebody's land under some lord who is full of benevolence and supports people like us. In places like that,
nobody has to be in distress. But to have to work with one's
hands and feet, and get one's living by one's own efforts —
this is all just too bad a custom! It is better not to make all
sorts of plans in your mind. Just behave in the proper way.
Don't work too ostentatiously, or let it seem as if you are
working too hard. If you do happen to possess two or three
old clothes, throw them away and put on some old sacking.
We are poor people with no one to make our complaints to.
We wander about without anywhere to stand or sit. So we
just go on weeping and weeping and praying for someone
to pity us. We have no words to express what we feel to
those in this world who are compassionate.'

People who think like that have made themselves poor
and pass through life in an impoverished state, in spite of
the advantages they have. They can only be considered as
being in a desperate state. Rinzai Daishi criticised such
people when he said: 'Self-indulgent people become
people of low class.' They are like fish who swim in the
water but grumble that they cannot see what the water
looks like. Or they are like birds who fly about in the air

but grumble because they have not found any method for seeing what the air looks like. People like that simply do not see that throughout all the ten regions of the universe there is no place where the absolute is not, nor that there is no sentient being which does not possess the wondrous law nature. I cannot help being sorry for those who, whilst walking in the midst of the one wondrous law and the pure land[38] of calm and light, have become one-sidedly attached to this transient world during their life here. They delude themselves into thinking that there are crowds of sentient beings, and that there is a hell after this life, so they weep and worry on account of their belief that that hell is infinite. They therefore cast away their hopes, thinking that those hopes are unreasonable and that the wondrous buddha-mind is unattainable, even though it is flowing before their very eyes, even though it never ceases to be clear and bright behind them and before them.

And all this distress comes about because they pass their lives vainly, relying on ideas that are mere illusions of sense-consciousness. It is also a sad thing that though there is the sutra of the Wondrous Law which provides a delightful taste of nirvana and has no superior in this world, it is placed with all sorts of secular books on the shelves of the revolving library and is allowed to crumble away there in the dark without being of any use or benefit to anyone, simply because there is no one who practises its teaching. And on that account people mistake the hell realms for the pure land, and the three evil hell states for the six stages of sentient existence.

Then somebody may perhaps ask me: 'When you speak about this teaching, what actual form of the teaching are you thinking of? Is it the four doctrines about paradise? Or is it the doctrine about the five ranks[39] of disciples of the

Lotus Law Sutra?' My answer is, 'No! It is not that sort of thing.' What I wish to emphasise is the particular portion of the *Lotus Sutra* which deals with accommodated truth, where it tells us that the beginning of buddhahood is the way of knowledge of the truth, and that is why bodhisattvas make their appearance in this world of ours. They appear here — that is the main point. All the *tathagatas* who have entered this world have expounded the inestimable and eternal dharma, and in every case their purpose has been to open up the understanding of all sentient beings to the knowledge of the Buddha.

If, therefore, sentient beings in this world give up the hope of obtaining buddha-knowledge, it will not make any difference to them what dharma they practise, for there will be no possibility of being united with the real purpose of the Buddha. The beginning of this buddha-knowledge is the discovery of the wondrous law of the one mind. But, unfortunately, in this final world age, which is the age of dissolution, this very dharma — the wondrous law of the one mind — is being discarded everywhere, and each person is now thinking just as he individually wishes to think. Sometimes it seems as if the real desire to know the truth is there — almost as it were by chance — but it soon turns out to be nothing but a sort of philosophical discussion or an elegant fashion of talk; and it is not worth thinking about such talk at all.

In the *Mahavairocana-abhisambodhi Sutra (Dainichi Sutra)* it says: 'For the absolute truth one must know one's own self.' But no one today pays any attention to that.

When people do not follow the dharma of the *Lotus Sutra* and do not know where the wondrous law is, but rather wander about saying it is in the west or it is in the east, and spend their days in great agitation talking about this or that being the buddha-way, they may be compared to the sons in the following allegory.

A very rich man, after experiencing a great deal of hardship and difficulty, had obtained a limitless estate of land and fields. This man one day said to his sons: 'You go now and become rich like me.' Then he distributed his excess property to them all equally, without any favouritism. But the sons did not follow their father's ways. They went wandering off into foreign countries. Some became beggars, standing at people's doorways. Some said they were mirror polishers and carried polishing stones about with them. Some said they would drive off birds which ate the millet grains in the fields. Others boasted about being the sons of a millionaire, forgetting about their own beggar-like appearance; and they treated other people with contempt. Still others did nothing but turn over the leaves of their ledgers, without having any notion of what their own property or fields looked like. And there were some amongst them who said that as long as they had their account books with them, there was nothing for them to fear. So they did anything that came into their heads, no matter how evil it might be. Some, again, said that they knew the correct manners of the rich, and even whilst they were starving and dying of thirst, carried on emulating the manners of those rich people. Some who knew nothing about their properties did nothing but shout out about them by day and night, and still others who perhaps realised just a little about the great value of their lands, became proud and proceeded to embark on lives of dissipation. So there was not a single one of those sons who conformed to their father's wishes.

In this story, the land and property represent the wondrous law of the one mind. The account books and ledgers represent the sutras. Those who went about begging at people's doors are those who listen to the teachings of various people — though the great business of learning to know how to approach buddhahood is, of course, to know one's self even if that entails suffering and patience in cold and heat — so these men only learn things which have no real substance in them, and yet they say that they have attained enlightenment.

People like that are the foolish persons mentioned in the *Lotus Sutra*, are they not? In the Mahayana scriptures even men who are holy and have attained the four results, are spoken of as ordinary men of the two vehicles. If attainment is such a simple and plain thing as people say it is nowadays — not bound up with ropes and vines — why did the Buddha shut himself up in those snowy Himalaya mountains for six years and discipline his body until he was nothing but skin and bone, so emaciated that he was like a brick tied round with thread, his knees as thin as reeds or rushes, his elbows piercing through his skin — and yet was not conscious of his state of emaciation? And when lightning struck down oxen and horses right in front of his eyes, he did not notice it because he was in such distress himself — until he at long last became the very first to open out the buddha-way of knowledge. What was all that about? Does it mean that the buddha-way was difficult in olden times but has become easy in our times? Was it like roasting ivy beans or boiling millet — something very hard at first but soft afterwards? If today's ease is right, then yesterday's hardness was wrong. But if yesterday's hardness was right, then today's ease is wrong. The bitter taste of ancient days was a very bitter taste. Nevertheless, the Buddha had only turned the wheel of the dharma for a very little time when things began to happen — the lightning struck, the stars fell, great Buddhist sages and patriarchs began to appear. He had but to pass through a place for such things to come to pass. But if today's ease is commendable, it is very easy. It is as easy as just looking at the portraits of wise men, or sages, or priests. Nevertheless, when people turn the wheel today, the captured fish stays still behind the bamboo fishnet, the injured tortoise stays lying on its back just as it was before. The one-eyed mule climbs up into the frozen corner of the rice fields, just as it did before — even when you pass by.

Which will you have? Today's ease or yesterday's hardness? And do not talk about this being the last age of the universe, for the ancients knew as well as we do, that in the final age both the *dhyana* teaching and the correct doctrine would perish from the world. It has often been said that it is a cause of grief that people should look for the wondrous law as if they could find it on discoloured paper, or that they should attach the true teaching to mere verbal argumentation. If this important matter could really have been accomplished by putting it down on pieces of paper or handing it down in traditions, then the mystic light would never have been shut off, nor would the feet of mystery have been injured. The head of the dharma-body *(dharma-kaya)*, would never have swelled, nor would the light of the dharma have had to shed tears. If people would make up their minds determinedly and definitely to recite the sacred formula ceaselessly by day and night so that they might continuously have the vision of the real law blossom (in their hearts), then there would be no need for anyone to go into the snowy Himalaya mountains, nor would they have to let their heads swell, for the blossom of the essential wondrous law would open out for them to see.

What is really essential for us to do, is to decide never to put aside our purpose until we see the vision of the wondrous law in our own minds. But we shall not receive anything more precious than we hope for. Even the World Honoured One, the Tathagata, before he saw the vision of the wondrous law in his own mind, was no different from any of us ordinary mortals revolving round the wheel. He was born, he died, he came, he went, but after he had seen the vision of the wondrous law in his own mind when he was up in those Himalaya mountains, he, for the first time in all the cycles, completed the true enlightenment.

And now, continuing with the explanation of our story, the sons who were polishing tiles and bricks, represent those persons who recognise the non-discriminating knowledge of the eighth consciousness or superconsciousness *(alaya-vijnana)*. They understand about the original dignity of the self, and think that, provided they have no illusions, they have already attained the buddha-mind, which is as clear as a mirror. But a mirror reflects all objects as they are — a crow appears black, a heron looks white, a willow is green and flowers are red. A mirror does not make any mistake of that sort. Nevertheless, from time to time one must wipe off carefully all the dust and dirt so that not the slightest trace of dust is left. All delusions must be swept away by day and night. These persons we are thinking of now, feel that they have to polish their tiles as carefully as birds picking up grains of millet. What they are actually doing, however, is called 'recognising' that there is a self — so there is no shining forth of light to brighten the hills and valleys. There was a good deal of this sort of thinking in ancient China, and the reason the patriarch Nangaku went and sat in front of Baso's hermitage and polished a tile there, was that he wished to teach that disciple this lesson. In the sage Chosha's *gatha*, he says: 'The reason that people who are studying the Way do not recognise the truth, is because they continue to acknowledge a self. Such people call that which is the origin of the everlasting kalpas or ages of existence of life and death, "the Original or Primeval Man".' It was for this reason that sages like Ji-myo, Shin-jo, So-kwo, Dai-e, and others, gritted their teeth and exerted the utmost limits of their strength to get rid of this idea. I need not mention here all the other teachers who have held the true doctrine on this matter. There has never been any Buddhist patriarch in all the three ages and in all the ten regions who has lacked this discernment, nor any sage or holy man. It is the ancient and unchangeable foundation of the teaching. And when I say 'discernment', what I mean is perception of the dignity of the Law of the Lotus. If people do all sorts of things as if they were the Way of Buddha. but have not this hope (of ridding themselves of the idea of a 'soul'), they may be compared to children scrambling on to a ship without any pilot, not knowing what country they want to go to, some rowing in one direction, others in another or opposite direction, pushing their oars this way and that merely in accordance with their own whims — yesterday rowing with the tide towards the east, today rowing with it towards the west — until in the end they are never able to escape from the boundless ocean. But if a pilot who knows the way, comes on board, sets the compass and fixes the course, they may reach the desired haven within a day. This pilot is the will to discern. The compass is the correct dharma. The helm is the moral discipline of the will.

Unfortunately, in this rowing of the boat into the harbour of the wondrous law, people insist on rowing outward — always outward — which means they are always looking

for the Buddha outside themselves. Or they look for a
patriarch or for nirvana or a pure land. Their method is to
look outwards — not inwards into their own minds —
which is why the more they seek, the further off they get;
the more they enquire, the more distant it all seems.

The real seekers are not like that at all. They have discovered what the wondrous law really is in their own existence — so they do not seek for an outward Buddha or patriarch. They do not think that the wondrous law is inside or
outside or in between, or that it is green, yellow, red or
white; and they persevere until they have assuredly had the
vision of it once. Boldly and courageously they never
cease by day or night, whether standing or sitting, sleeping
or waking; they never give up until they have accomplished their purpose, pressing ever on (maintaining
the correct spirit of meditation). Day and night they dili-
gently investigate, sometimes going over the problems
again and again so as to perceive what the matter really is.
They must go on at all costs — for this is what we call 'the
Dharma which bites into the Lion-Man'. But if one does
not see the wondrous law in one's own mind — if one
merely goes on asking what the wondrous law is — that is
like chasing Chinese dogs with clods of earth!

So, put aside everything else and become one who has
no outside ideas whilst you repeat the sacred formula
namu myo ho renge kyo — *'Hail Wondrous Law of the
Lotus Blossom Sutra'.*

If you think that I have anything else I can give you —
some other teaching more acceptable about the dharma —
you are making a grave mistake.

Namu Myo Ho Renge Kyo. Namu Myo Ho Renge Kyo.

Dated this Fourth Year of Enkyo (1747), the Fourth Calendar Sign (Hinoto) the year of the Hare, the Twenty-Fifth Day, Midwinter.

You may, I am afraid, find the above long letter troublesome to read, but if you read it out to the people in your hermitage, that will be a meritorious work. At least, it is with that wish that I have written this letter. It may, by good fortune, help you to see the vision of the wondrous law in your own heart, so go on constantly repeating your own sacred formula — that is my heart's desire for you.

(25th Midwinter day of the Hare. Fourth Sign Era of Entei.)

Sermons to his Peasant Parishioners

The Awakening from Daydreaming

Shinkoku No Mezame

(Abridged translation)

Nobody likes ordinary, commonplace things. And that is quite natural. A good medicine is bitter to the taste, but it wakes us up. It makes us open our eyes. And waking up spoils our dreams.

Everybody likes what is new, the novelty of things. The world-bridge which takes us across the floating transient world of ours so lightly, is dangerous for the feet which walk over it. And it is not sufficient to tell people to keep to the middle of the road. The road is broad. Open your eyes!

If you open your eyes, you will find that whatever enterprise you are undertaking on the stage of this life will appear in an entirely new light. You will see the three thousand worlds all at one glance.

Some time ago I felt a strong urge to go and see what the great city of Yedo looked like. Oh, what a great city it is! It is indeed a great and flourishing city, but it is forsaking the three ancient forms of the Buddha's teaching. In one way this seemed to be quite opportune for me, for fortunately the new jewels which I wish to sell can be stored in a house rented in a back street, and I need only to wait for good prices.

Come and buy! Come and buy! There is plenty put away in my chests. If you like my wares just ask for them. This is a wholesale jeweller whose treasures are priceless, but buy them for yourselves.

Everything under heaven seems to be in tangled confusion, especially the things of this world. People must take the past and future into their own hands and look at the truth. They must try to see it with their own eyes — the false and the correct, the good and the bad.

There are many self-existences, gods and buddhas; and there are many teachings connected with the many deities. A thousand yen, ten thousand yen, will not be sufficient for you.

The Confucian scholar and the Buddhist teacher are like seed. If you do not know which is the right seed, it will bring forth nothing but leaves and branches, nothing but inessential things for you. And that is not surprising because our eyes and noses and all our senses are nothing but obstructions.

People *are* apt to rely on their eyes, noses, ears, tongues, and bodies; and for that very reason it is difficult for them to control their hearts. The heart, therefore, is left in darkness. A Confucian scholar makes literature his life's work. He picks up the dregs of the ancients; and he thinks it well to compose poems. But he scatters rhetorical flourishes up and down in his writings almost haphazardly, all the time having no idea what his master's face was like, nor what his intentions were — those intentions which the master himself carried out so well when it was a matter of goodness, or of heaven's will. What the scholar does is nothing more than give help in a dream to a dream. In the lectures which he sometimes delivers, he gives literal explanations out of the delusion of his own ideas of wisdom. When he lectures on that great saying of Confucius — 'Piercing through to everything from the One' — the lecturer speaks many words with his mouth but never will anything be heard from the clear vision of his heart.

Scholarship of this sort is nothing but an ear for seeking abstractions. Much learning and many arts lead merely to the delusions which are rank growing seeds of phantasy. Scholarship is nothing but this.

What is the originating source of joy, anger, sorrow, and pleasure in one's own heart? True scholarship is first of all the learning of how to use one's eyes, ears, nose, tongue, and body correctly, and also how to use one's hands and feet for their proper work. When one reaches the true understanding of this, one is a self-existing being, a buddha. When one has done that, one's heart is subjugated and one's body is disciplined. One's home will then be properly regulated. It is this which is the foundation for governing the land and the whole world. This is true discipline and learning. So, everybody, please wake up. When you wake up, you are lord of heaven and earth. Right round the clock you will be used by self-existence, the Buddha. But if you do not realise this, there will arise a pride of self, a sense of dissatisfaction, of folly. It is dangerous not to realise this.

Turn now and look at the Buddhist religious life. It seems to aim at cupidity and fame because of the depth of its secular outlook. It takes interest in money-matters and property. Some priests of low spiritual power conduct themselves even worse than do many secular persons. The Buddha's teaching has utterly fallen to the ground. Shakyamuni's real intentions are no longer understood. That 'Voice of One Hand' of Buddha, those nine years of meditation whilst facing the wall by Daruma, yes, and even that smile on the face of the Buddha[40] (whilst on the Vulture Peak) with the plucked flower in his hand — one can hardly believe it — but all this has been entirely cast away as into the Western sea. The priests all try to keep in the good graces of their patrons and almsgiving parishioners. They seldom look at the Buddhist teachings or the records of the patriarchs. All they do is just lick up the dregs of the teachings of the ancients. And when they do occasionally preach and lecture, speaking as though the ideas had come out of their own hearts, their breasts are full of the three poisons and the five lusts, so they do nothing but scatter about illusions and vain doctrines in the world. They climb up onto their lecture seats with looks of triumph so as to fascinate and bedevil the men and women who come to hear them. Without any feelings of shame, they come to an agreement with their lusts which are so hard to suppress. This is a case of 'one blind man leading many to the hell-like states'.

So, everybody, open your eyes! Wake up! Turn your hearts right over. Do not lose your way amongst the sense objects of this world. Polish the mirrors of your natural hearts, brighten them up. Don't follow the bad customs of these times. In these days there has grown up a custom amongst worldly people who have no true wisdom, to exchange gods for buddhas and buddhas for gods, to use incantations, magic, and long prayers. Some even go so far as to light fires for the purpose of making incantations and invocations, and as a result new illusions are apt to arise. And many people, suffering from some grief or disease, go about asking different gods to help them. They ask: 'Is there some special Yakushi Nyorai (Medicine Buddha) in some particular shrine who may be useful for my special sickness?' Or, 'What Jizo is there near here who may be good for these pains in my stomach?' Or, 'Perhaps there is some Kannon who is good for headaches.' Or, 'Perhaps this particular Fudo is good for such and such.' Moreover, they combine their worldly pleasures and needs with their religion, just as if they were going to enjoy a flower show. When they make vows they do so with disordered hearts. Their world is the transient world where there is no end to their lusts. When they have possessions, they desire still more. Even when they have more than they know what to do with, they still feel that they do not have enough. They think that they can ask the gods and buddhas for any unreasonable thing and that they will be given whatever their lusts desire. But surely if the gods and buddhas wished to do so, the very trees and shrubs and the very earth itself would speak out for them.

Everybody should know that Yakushi Nyorai is nothing other than a manifestation of that power which saves from pain, answering to the inward desire for healing, which all sentient beings feel in this transient and illusionary world. And 'Jizo' means simply that the depths of the mind are very deep indeed. They are, as it were, 'stored in the ground'. (NB The ideogram 'ji' means 'ground' and 'zo' means 'store', so this is a kind of pun on the name 'Jizo'.) Moreover, the outward form of Jizo's image is of a gentle aspect, to show how good the inner nature of the mind is.

'Kannon', too, signifies simply the ideas of seeing and hearing. ('Kan' is the ideogram for 'perception', and 'on' is the ideogram for 'sound'. Kannon is the one who perceives and hears the sounds or prayers of all sentient beings.)

All these can be summarised in our Zen teaching about the 'voice or sound of one hand'. If one understands the meaning of this, then one is truly awake. And if one is truly awake, then the whole world is Kannon.

And look at the image of Fudo who is so much in fashion these days. It is meant to be a manifestation of the five duties of life.[41] The rope which hangs on his left arm symbolises the tying up of the illusions of sentient beings so that these illusions may not operate. The sword which he holds in his right hand shows that he cuts off all illusionary ideas of sentient beings. The flame which rises behind him is the symbol of the burning up of illusions. He is standing on the great earth, which shows that he is treading down all illusions so that they may not rise up into the minds of sentient beings. The pure water falling at his side is for the purpose of purifying all illusions. The aspect of his body is that of a fierce deity whose right eye looks up towards heaven, and whose left eye looks down towards the earth. He is standing like an awe-inspiring warrior. All this is an allegory, telling people not to wander away in the senses of this illusionary and transient world.

Gods and buddhas have in reality no form, and as they have no form they are unknown to those who dwell in the realms of the secular life. They have been given form out of necessity. But do not rely on names and forms. If you do, that is illusionary. Not even the buddhas of Embudangon[42] have any other origin than on this earth, which is nothing but an accumulation of impurities.

So, everybody, wake up! When you wake up you will find that this whole world, above and below, is nothing other than a regarding of oneself. Find out what your mind really is and open your eyes in true wakefulness. If you must worship gods and buddhas make sure that your heart is pure and also your body. Be humble and have a calm mind with no vain thoughts or illusions in it. Then you will attain to the condition of 'non-self'.[43]

That is a summary of this teaching. No matter how little sickness there may be in your body there is pain in your heart when there is illusion in your mind. This is the chronic sickness of all sentient beings. It was to save us from this that Shakyamuni walked through the land barefooted helping people. If you do reach the condition of non-self, you must not therefore become foolish doers of evil. This non-self is nothing other than the stopping of one's own painfully narrow thinking, and the preserving of the heavenly and natural truth which is called 'the eye of the teaching'. The ordinary person is apt to be sunk deep in his self-lusts which invite evils and disasters. Be thoroughly discriminating in this matter. When natural calamities befall us, it is all right to pray to gods and buddhas, but in that case the gods and buddhas are only the targets of our prayers. Do not let your mind be taken captive by the target. Keep your body firm and do not let your thoughts be absorbed by anything. Let your mind be calm, and fix your attention quietly and clearly, and then the arrow which you shoot will never miss its mark. But if your mind is distracted, even a target of only five feet away may be missed. What is important is to hit the target and it does not matter much what the target is, great or small. Be sure in your own mind about this.

Takamagahara, the Shinto land of the gods, is my own mind. The Pure Land of Amida is my own mind. Every pure place is a place where the gods and buddhas dwell. So be sure not to have an evil spot in your mind. Hatred, ill will, and such things, are the 'stock-funds' of places of hell. They are the seed of the five lusts, of illusion and impurity. When there is illusion the mind becomes clouded and does not know the truth. Perplexities then arise, and because of these perplexities great loss occurs. Such a state of affairs in the mind is disliked by the gods and buddhas, and that is why the sages and holy men say that in such cases, it is useless to trouble divine beings.

There is a saying: 'Hear the Way in the morning and die in the evening.' That is perhaps too brutal a way to put it, but it is undoubtedly true. If someone can live for, say, five or ten years and perform the way which he has learned, that is something he may well rejoice in. Our lives are very short and our bodily lives much limited, so do not be negligent. Put your whole heart into this business of carrying out the duties of the Way. This is what I beg of you all to do.

There is no merit or virtue which comes merely for the asking. This is the great Way in which one does not argue about loss or gain. Look at the ideogram for 'virtue'; it is composed of two parts: one part means 'straight' and the other part means 'heart' or 'mind'. The straight heart or mind is the truth of heaven and it is called 'integrity'. Every man who is the vassal of a lord must be particularly careful to be straight and correct without self-will. He must be wholeheartedly his lord's man, nor may he be one-sided in his loyalty. One who is correct in these ways and observes the law of heavenly truth, is loyal. Such people should not hope for important advantages for themselves. The one word 'perseverance' is all the 'capital-stock' or fund which they need for accomplishment. Keep on persevering. That is the one great thing to do. And whether one is a high vassal or a mere nobody, so long as one keeps on persevering, heaven will pour down blessings on one. And look at the ideogram for 'straight'. It also is made up of two parts: one part means 'unity' and the other part means 'stop'. If you 'stop' with 'one' simple heart you will be an upright person, at one with integrity. When the very roots of our hearts are whole, integrated, at one with their true nature, then they are 'stopped' at 'unity'. Though heaven is high, crouch down! Though the earth is hard, tread on it softly! Great things are destroyed by little things. An embankment of a thousand miles may crumble and fall because of one little frog's hole in it. If you are careless about little things, you will accomplish nothing. Everybody — Wake up!

Looking back over the history of ancient and modern times there has not been any country — whether China during the Tang dynasty, or our own Japan — which has rejoiced in peace and order. Think of the age of our Emperor Nintoku (313-399) when palace and cottage slept in all quietness with high pillows. All the land had peace and everybody had a fat belly. The cities had plenty of gold and jewels, make-believe jewels. Wise men and fools alike dressed softly and luxuriously. Tea houses and boatmen's houses flourished. It was all like an imitation paradise. But it was really a great hell. Crowds of men and women were all the time being pushed into extreme perplexity until in the end there came great distress upon all of them.

Many people bear a grudge against this transient world. They do not realise that even this world is better than they themselves have deserved to reach. They talk, too, about the Buddha, but they don't know what the Buddha is. Indeed, the Buddhas are for them only something to make use of. Fortunate are they if by one chance in a thousand they are able to take advantage of a little of the instruction which can be found in the world of mankind.

I am afraid that this long discourse may have been wearying to you. The measure of words is like the seas and the mountains — nothing but an overflow of delusions. They should all be shut up in one tiny mustard seed. And then there would be nothing — no rice, no goods for sale in the store. I have to write this from sheer necessity, and my essay is not in good order because of my other occupations.

In conclusion, I wish to express my felicitations to you all. 'The sound of a rough gale in a new jewel.'

> Dated the first year of Non-Attachment[44] in the era of Non-Separative cycle. The day of the full moon of the Absolute and Identity of the Several Vehicles. The second year of Kwan-Ei (1749). The fourth calendar sign of the Horse. The fourth month. The day of the birth of the Buddha (eighth day of the fourth month). The place of writing: The Universe where Reality and Phenomena are conjoined, the Land of Non-Birth. The County of Wonders. The Village of Stopping.[45] The Temple of the Real Aspect of all the Dharmas.

> Written by the Chief Priest of the Hall of Vision, a disciple of Thunder, Light, and Morning Dew. Subject of the Essay: Entry to the Way of the Cell of the Mirage Flowers in the Sky. A disciple of the great teacher Ippen of the Temple of Throwing Away Life and Destroying the Body. Corrected and edited by Purity Alone of the Cell of Non-Difficulty in the Monastery of the Dharma World and the Temple of Aspects. And a disciple of the Priest All Aspects and Non-Aspects in the Temple of Immovability and Sincerity.

The Plain-Looking Courtesan's Ballad of Bravado

Otafuku Joro No Kobiki Uta

A courtesan constant! An egg square!
A moonlight night on the last day of the month!

Everybody talks all the time about the will of heaven. It is hateful to be censured by heaven.

Love letters, lots of love letters. Often they are lovelorn letters. But I don't like temporary flowers. I am afraid of the very idea of having lots of men. I am sorry, too, for those who are good looking.

People praise me for my good looks, and they say that I who sleep alone and don't like men, kill life. I do not kill. Yoichi of Nasu may kill with the point of his spear. Many kill with their bright eyes.

There may be lots and lots of gentlemen, but for me there is only one beloved one.

The ditty sung by an old woman may be entertaining, but she may not be able to play a tune on a flute. It is all right to sing when one knows the tune, but be careful what you sing if your guest be an unrefined boor.

Down, down, prostrate yourselves. The seven Buddhas[46] are coming. Shakyamuni is coming too. Just listen for a little while. You will remember the most important things. If you are yearning for life you may be throwing it away. Old men and women, listen to the words of my ditty.

Everything that we do is impermanent. This is the law of life-death, and of the cessation of life and the cessation of death. It is the discovery of the happiness of nirvana. You may not know it, but the great Kobo Daishi disentangled the skein for us and put it into his *'I Ro Ha Ni Ho He To'*.[47] If you can't find it there, then listen to the drum minstrel who puts the big and little things all together in his songs.

Really and truly this passing world is a fickle place, isn't it? We, men and women, mountains, rivers, the sun, the moon, morning and evening, bamboos, trees, the whole earth — no sooner has the flower bloomed than it falls. No sooner is a thing completed than it fails. No sooner is one born than one dies. Everything which exists comes to nought. And yet! And yet! Don't we all of us think that we are going to be in this world for a very long time, as if for thousands and ten thousands of years?

But while we are loitering here and there, lingering about or tramping around, the hurricane of impermanence suddenly bursts upon us. We know not when or where. Strong men who seem as if they might overcome demons in wrestling matches, beautiful maidens who look like angels — not one of them can step aside out of the path of the storm. All of them come to the time when they have to draw their last breath.

So it seems as if the four great fundaments of which our bodies are composed return to nothingness and that only one thing is left — and that is the mind. The good and evil things which we have done during our life have no outward shape. They do not turn into earth or ashes, but they lead us onwards. Good works lead us to a good place; bad works lead us to a bad place. The stage screen changes. We put on different stage dresses. All this is in accordance with the law of karma. There are the six abodes — heaven, the human realm, hell, the world of hungry ghosts and so on.[12] People are reborn as cows or horses. They are born, they die. Nothing is settled. For the truth is that there is no permanence anywhere, not even in our acts and words. This is the law of life-death.

If your own minds do not assure you of these truths, then follow the teachings of the buddhas and bodhisattvas. Set yourselves to carry out correctly their rules and teachings. Cut off and destroy in yourselves the roots of avarice, anger, ignorance, pride. When you have cut off and destroyed the life-death of the 'six worlds', as it is called, that will be the cessation of both life and death. When you reach that stage, your mind will come to an end and there will be real peace — the calm of non-attachment to forms and shapes of the world. Then the moon will be your pillow, so peacefully will you sleep. The sky will be your couch, and you will command a view of the lotus storeworld of Amida and Vairocana. Your body and mind will be pure. Everything will be pure. This is the first entry into nirvana. Then you will find yourselves rubbing shoulders with Shakyamuni, Avalokiteshvara (Kannon), and Jizo (Kshitigarbha). Then you will find yourselves rowing the boat of the Vow which ferries sentient beings across the river to the nirvana shore. Then you will be able to go about teaching the divine mysteries in all the ten regions of the universe. Then you will bring salvation to father, mother, brothers and sisters, uncles and aunts, those still living in the world and those who from unbegotten eternity may still be wandering painfully in the six realms. You will be able to guide every one of them away from old age, sickness, and death, away from the roots and branches of ever-recurring existence. And you will be able to enthrone them on the calyx, glorious with the seven treasures, where delicious foods of a hundred flavours will be provided for them. There you and they will be clothed like heavenly beings, according to your heart's desire. There you will be in the company of hosts of angels. There your ears will be charmed with the most marvellous music. There you will be able to rejoice in the sight of the variegated flowers which come down from heaven. In short, you will become buddhas. Oh, wouldn't you like that? Don't you long for that?

If you are not entirely averse to these joys, then just listen again. This mind which we all possess is what is important. It must be kept firm and resolute. It may bring forth a buddha, or it may build up a hell. It is the most untrammelled and wicked fellow. So do not let anyone be careless about it. In this transient world of ours it is not only old men and women who must be careful. Healthy, young, strong men and women can never know what may happen to these bodies of ours, even before this very night falls. It is foolish to be careless about it. Whether one likes it or not, the aged and the young alike may have to throw off their lives at any moment. But although we all of us know this, we prefer to look the other way. If we could see some shape or form of our mind, riotous with the five lusts reflected in a mirror, it would be a repulsive sight from top to bottom. Men, after long ages of rebirth, at last come to birth in this world of men, and then they behave like hungry demons, or like lower grades of demons. They never stop striving for fame. From morn to eve, in high ranks and low ranks there is the lust for property and the lust for sensual pleasure. The whole heart is clouded and the bright world becomes dark. Oh, so dark, dark, dark! It becomes the black land of the senses. The original Amida and the Buddha who dwell in us are painted over with the impurities of the ten wickednesses and the eight falsities[48] until at last they are so splashed and smarmed over, that they cannot be recognised. And it is we ourselves, who with our own hands do this. We build up our own hells. It is the false or non-buddha-nature in us that does this.

The non-buddha-nature shows itself in those who hold to the false view that keeps them attached to the idea that this body is utterly brought to an end at its death, or that this realm, and with it this body, will continue into inexhaustible eternity. It is the nature which thinks itself smart and clever in its worldly wisdom. It is a state of spiritual laziness. It has no discernment of the law of karma, and selfishly indulges in the three poisons and five lusts. It indolently and insolently denies — both by the views it holds and by its words — Shakyamuni's teaching about the ten rules[49] the five rules,[50] purifying the six roots[51] as taught also in the veneration of the goddess Amaterasu, and the five human relationships,[52] and five eternal virtues[53] as taught by Confucius. People in this class are the ones whom the Buddha spoke of as being non-buddha-natures. There are large numbers of this class in this world, and the hell realms are crowded with them.

There is no end to what I might say about these hells. And, everybody, this is not a matter for other people to think about. It is our own affair. For it is our own minds which are like the green room in a theatre, so changeful are our minds. In these we may see all sorts of changes going on, like the jugglery of ball throwing, the ball passing quickly from one hand to the other, from right to left. How quickly does the glance of one's eye alter? At one minute the polite and courteous look when one is in the presence of a high-ranking person, changes to the hypocritical look when one is in the presence of one's own lord or parent. The fond look when one is with one's favourite child. Pleasant as Jizo when borrowing money in the morning; angry and distorted, like Enma when going to repay it in the evening. Pride and insolence in a temple where there is no resident priest. Perverted flattery deceiving one's own self. Rebellion against the teaching of the way of heaven. Murder, unmercifulness, self-pleasing in one's tastes. Providing for one's own family at the cost of other people's lives. Injuring and causing distress to others without feeling that there is anything wrong in so doing. Not judging the feelings of others, though one has one's own feelings. The mind which thinks it can pass through this world only by getting money. Even when it does not do so by breaking through walls, it does so by dishonest exchanges made on the abacus and with the writing brush. Knowing how to rob the gods. Forgetting the benefits received from one's lord or from one's parents. Living the life of cat and dog in one's own family. Mothers-in-law glaring at daughters-in-law; daughters-in-law making faces at mothers-in-law. Insincerity and unfilial conduct, like a fire spreading and starting other fires by evil-speaking and gossip. Husbands pretending that they are not 'drawing two bows at the same time'. Housewives using two measures, and then when burnt a little in one place, becoming green with jealousy until their very bosoms burn with it. And when the flame of jealousy flares up, being maddened into frenzy, so that horns seem to grow on their heads. But to go and hang or drown oneself is not much of an honour, is it?

And then, again, if one's own opinions are not accepted by people at once, one begins to slander, insinuate, boast and say that people are all against you. Both parties soon become angry and try to deprecate the other, and talk about 'mine, theirs, his, hers, this, cackle, cackle, quarrel, quarrel', and so it goes on until hatred and the desire to hurt pile up into a great heap. At last cutting and slashing begins. Or there is addiction to gambling, carousals, unrestrained drinking bouts, until real crimes take place which shorten the life of fathers and mothers — everything seems to be done in utter recklessness.

All these things are sowing the seeds of the hells. Even if people have done good deeds in past existences and owing to the merit accumulated have now reached the stage of birth in this world of mankind, for those who do the sort of things just referred to, the hells of the future are fixed. And that is why the Buddha is so full of pity. All living beings in this world have received some benefit or other from father or mother in previous worlds, and now they want to repay their benefactors in some way. But no matter how much they may wish to help those who have helped them in the past, no one can escape from the evil which they have created for themselves by their own actions. The seeds sown are seeds sown in the mind, and these seeds come up in unexpected places — here one, there ten thousand — and each must reap the pains and griefs of eternity.

If you do not want to reap those seeds, then from this very day and moment, cut straight back to the fundamental nature in yourselves. Study and accept the truth of the divine teaching of the Buddha, and the holy ones and sages. Be careful to observe the precepts of filial piety, of brotherliness, of loyalty and fidelity. Do not be careless about the state of faith in your mind. Lead a disciplined life. Surely this is not too difficult for you…

(Here follow lessons from the birds and fish, which are also given in the Drum Minstrel's Song. q.v.)

All these things, the little birds and fishes teach you, and you can see them every day, but you don't keep your eyes fixed on them. You don't let your ears retain the lessons. You lose your self-respect when you find that you are of lower moral degree even than the birds and four-footed creatures.

If we really understand what our true personal dignity is, we would at once spring to our feet and change our very hearts and minds. We would revere the three treasures and the patriarchs. We would put filial piety first and above all else. We would preserve that proper and respectful love between husband and wife. We would be cordial in the courtesy of our behaviour towards our brothers and sisters, and friends. We would never forget our duty of fidelity towards our relatives and neighbours. We would have compassion for the sick and the poor. We would work with all our might for our home and family. We would be obedient to the ordinances of our rulers. We would be merciful, honest and patient, so as to be good examples to others. Then, without appearing to instruct, we would in the most natural way be able to act as guides. Then all classes of people would associate in peace. Everyone would pass through life with smiling faces, cooperating with the Buddha and the gods of heaven and earth.

Then the eight million gods, Bonten (Brahma), Taishakuten (Indra), Daikoku, Bishamonten — all of them would be a protection to you. Evil demons and false gods would flee. There would be no sickness. The whole world would be at peace. The five harvest grains would mature and every home be prosperous. The children who were born would be good, too.

So, everybody! Don't forget to repeat the sutras morning and evening, or say the 'Hail Arhat' or the 'Hail Amida' or the Sutra of the Lotus. These are all swords to cut away the roots of ignorance. If you recite these words with sincerity and conviction, the words which come from your mouth will go into your ears, and the illusions will disappear, so that you will attain to the state of *samadhi*. Delight in the buddha-heart and the buddha-heart in delight! All this may come about without your having to leave the place where you happen to be. This is the true entry into the pure land.

And there is a nearer way, the way of correct meditation. Those who wish for this spirit of meditation should perform meditation on the great good and on wisdom. But do not think that this is like the proverbial *'botamochi'*, a cake that falls into the mouth from the shelf. It will not do so. It will not fill your stomach just because I tell you about it. Unless you drink water, you will not know whether it is cold or hot.

The six lower orders of sentient beings and the four higher orders have but one unchanging substance. If those who wish for this spirit of meditation can but perceive the one reality, they will understand that this transient world is indeed nothing other than an entry into light. If one goes wrong about this reality, then nothing is left but the three hell realms.

So I want to repeat over and over again: Do not be careless. When the hurricane of impermanence strikes, there will be no time to wait even a minute. Slowly but surely, one by one, past things are getting further away, future things are getting nearer, and when death comes, one or other kind of body will become fixed. So what is important, is never to forget that what is essential is enlightenment.

All the buddhas and bodhisattvas were at one time ordinary mortals like ourselves. They became enlightened and accomplished all the virtues perfectly; and now they are free to help all sentient beings to cross to the other shore. Therefore, let each one of us learn from them. Then, when you are actually at the treasure mountain you will not have to swing empty hands. Make sure of enlightenment. Don't wait until the drought before you dig your well. Listen, I beg you, to this great truth. Chew on it. Do not throw it away. Make up your mind and set your will to step out on the way of bodhi-knowledge.

The Drum Minstrel's Song of the Great Way

Dai Do Cho-Bo-Kure

Here he comes! Here he comes! Ah, Ah, he comes. Watch. He comes. Nothing less. Never Again. Down, down. Prostrate yourselves. Everybody listen carefully.

This fellow inside of us, which we call our mind, and which each one of us calls his own, this fellow has no eye or nose. He has no hand or foot. Dear me. Dear me. He is altogether a bad fellow. I need not tell you, but even if he were to live in this world for a thousand years — it may happen just when one is off one's guard, all of a sudden — look out, look out, the messenger of impermanence may come to fetch him. Won't that be a crisis? Ah, how flustered and agitated shall we be.

And even whilst we are being led off by this messenger, we still go on deceiving ourselves thinking that unless a man has money he is hardly to be considered a man. And from the top of our head to the soles of our feet, whether we are standing up or sitting down, we never forget about matters of lust and merit.

But, indeed, what good fortune it is that we should have come this once into this world of man, which is so hard to attain to in the cycle of existences, because we have here the great highway where there are five human relationships and the five cardinal virtues to be practised, things so highly regarded by holy men and sages. And it is a precious thing too for us to have the holy ones and sages to teach us and explain all about goodness and evil, falsity and truth, and to do it so fully and without adding or subtracting anything. We cannot count, we cannot add to or subtract from the days, months and years which have passed since the world came into existence, and nearer and nearer comes the end of the last age. So much, then, should the thirst for teachers of the Way increase. So much the more precious to us should be the gods and buddhas. So much more should their influence and authority increase. They should be as precious to us as the members of our own imperial family.

But just think, everybody, how fortunate if even a trifling bit of the vision of the Way is seen by us, that vision which mangles and cuts into small pieces those causes of evil — that vision for which the gods and buddhas dart about us and ripple round us in their love and compassion for us. How fortunate it is for us! So apply yourselves to this correct way with all possible industry and zeal.

What you all call 'evil' is no doubt murder or setting fire to people's houses, or stealing, and of course you do not do that sort of evil. Your ears are frozen when you listen to groundless falsehoods about hell and demons, after you hear of the death of someone by some 'fate'. And the white-robed layman fancies himself safe because he has his three meals a day like a man of high rank. And though he chatters away like a parrot or a monkey, he does not see the essential matters even in his dreams. He surrenders to 'reasoning and self', matters of words, without knowing the truth at all. And anyway, it would be no use at all if he did know the truth whilst his acts were evil.

If a sick man does not drink his medicine, why, even a famous physician like Henjaku[54] or a sage like Kiba[55] would have to throw up the sponge. And that is why Asendai and others have had to repeat over and over again until they were utterly weary, the message that not even the Buddha can bring salvation to any sentient being if that being has no affinity with buddhahood. And who is this Asendai? What has he done for us? Asendai is not something outside ourselves. People who ask who he is, are Asendais in embryo.

These things which I am speaking about are more precious than a pot of gold handed down in a family for ten generations, but they will be of no use at all when the crisis comes if one twists and crosses his words this way and that, trying to explain what one thinks. For the crisis is nothing other than this: It is when the messenger comes from the land of darkness. You may then hope to use logical arguments or to put your case in this way or that, but you will not be permitted to argue at all, for at that very instant the visor before the eyes of Enma will look very fine-meshed and no one will even expect to escape. You will be led away as a prisoner. That will be a terrible moment. If everybody is wriggling and wandering about in confusion in this present world, the future world will be a rough and fearsome time. And think of the poor gods and buddhas who want to help us in some way, but at that time what will they be able to do? Even if their tears of pity flow down like rivers, they will not be able to save us from the excess of evil which we have produced by our own acts during our lifetime.

So, everybody, never let yourselves be off guard.

Think of the fishes. There is that fellow we call the carp. He is a clever fellow. He climbs up waterfalls and the rapids of streams with a great 'heave and a ho', with a great push and a shove, and he nearly succeeds in becoming a dragon.

And the fox, too. He surprises us by jumping so lightly over the sacred Torii of Inari[56] and seems to become a deity himself.

We can also learn from the pigeon. He seems too stupid as he stoops and says 'coo, coo', but he is making his three polite bows of invitation and courtesy.

The sparrow's song tells us of the one way of loyalty, for what he chirps is the sound 'chu, chu', which in our language means 'loyalty'.

The raven with his 'caw, caw' practises his filial duty, for he feeds his parents; and his words in our language mean 'filial piety' *(koko)*.

All these creatures call and sing to us by day and night, but no one seems to listen to them. From dawn to dusk they sing. Ah, is it man alone who does nothing but whistle meaninglessly? Is it man alone who is so casual? Surely he will lose his self-respect if it can be said that he is less than the little fishes and the birds.

But you must not lose your self-respect. Get back to the source of your true nature, and don't forget to carry out your duties of filial piety — brotherliness, loyalty and faithfulness. Become true.

Really and truly there is no way of becoming a god or a buddha unless you start from your own true nature. And that should not be a difficult thing to do.

Old grandpa who cannot read his A B C, old grandma who cannot read the ideograms for 'compassion' or for 'long life' — it is no use for you to try to attain anything just by repeating the one word formulas like *'namu'*[57] or *'nyozegamon'*,[58] or to use long passages of the sutra about Amida. Rather than that, practise the three virtues of honesty, patience and kindness every day until it becomes easy to do, and carry on your religious duties too with every breath, without straining yourselves at all. And take the beads of your mala[59] into your hands and count them in the proper way, one hundred and eight times, one with each breath that you draw. Then your inner mind will become resplendent, for the body of Amida will be formed in you. He will be so close to you that you will be amazed.

All this sounds easy, but there is one unfortunate thing about it. This mind of ours changes so rapidly. It changes quicker than children playing a game. When you are in the presence of a great nobleman then your face shows polite looks, but in the presence of your creditors your face is like Enma's. This mind of ours is like a green-eyed monster; it changes so quickly. Where will it all end?

Or remember what we think about the weather. We speak of the rain, wind, thunder and lightning as part of heaven's regime and are very afraid and reverential about it at such times. But if the weather happens not to meet with our convenience, we curse and scold it. And that does not make the weather change. Or we point at the sun and moon in reverence and make enquiries of them, and yet we don't mind behaving in quite unseemly ways in their full view. There is nothing but impudence in the way we rebel against heaven and earth.

Such is what comes out of our opinionated minds, and there is nothing of the teaching of the Way in them.

Alas, alas, it is all very terrifying. What shall the likes of us do?

The above is Hakuin's chobokure [humorous parody]. Signed 'Author with the Heavenly Eye'.
Whether what is said above is true or not, he who can discriminate will know.
Here it has been transcribed by one seeking for the Divine Blessing. End.

The Lay of the Old Lady 'Heart Control'

Shushin Baba Kobiki Uta

Gracious are the mercies of heaven and earth. They give us the heat and cold, and the day and night, which do not come together. In the day one works; in the night one rests. By the grace of the rain and dew, the five grains ripen and so do the trees and herbs in the far off hills. And the benefits given us by our lords are higher than the mountains. The land is prosperous down to its lowest cottage and on and on for ten thousand ages. As the trees and shrubs bend and flutter in the wind, let not the benefits given us by our lords be forgotten. And the benefits given us by our parents too, are deeper than the ocean depths. The greater the filial piety, so much longer will that family flourish. Our parents are the field which produces wealth for us in this evanescent world. In spite of all this, many who have only a short opportunity to show their gratitude, run away from their proper duties.

One's body may be five feet high, but unless the heart inside it has control, that person is but an infant. Even the art and skill of a warrior is secondary to this controlling heart. Without that, the house is empty with foxes and badgers running about it.

There is a famous saying in the book of Dai Kobo of Mombu written during the era of the Sung dynasty in China. In a section about the three great duties of the warrior, the question is asked: 'What happens when a sudden and unexpected calamity occurs?' The reply is: 'Because the heart which should always be in control, is not always ready, the warrior's duty is to see that he so disciplines himself that his heart is always in control. His prowess with the bow may be such as that of Chinda Hachiro, with the spear that of a Mada, with the longsword that of a Kuro, but though even these men might have been deceived, at times of crisis it is the controlling heart alone which prevents one becoming a coward. There are not two supreme goods for the heart. He whose heart is rightly fixed, is better than the most intelligent and well-informed man in Japan or China.

To clothe his warriors in silk and provide them with good food is only one small part of the lord's business. There is the matter of instructing them in the many arts and other activities of life. But let us leave these matters aside for the time being and consider this matter of controlling the heart. The power to control the heart is truly something to be grateful for. The blade of the longsword and the edge of the shortsword cannot be compared with this. No arrow or gun can reach up to it. So it has no enemies of that sort. Everything may become the controlling heart within us: the sky, the sun, the moon, the sea, the mountains — yes, the very earth we stand on — all may become a heart to control us. This heart of ours is our Takamagahara (the Shinto land of the gods). It is the place where no five lusts, and no three poisons can penetrate. The building up of the nation in prosperity will only go on as long as this supreme good continues steadily.

Nor is this only a matter for warriors. Those who enter the religious life, learners of the dharma, priests and teachers, all of these, unless they have hearts which are steady and in control, are no better than ordinary mortals. Palace, cottage/cottage, palace — it is the controlling heart which marks the line of the tides. When people of high degree and low degree, all the tens of thousands of people, have their hearts in steady control, then we may say 'Banzai'. For such a world will need no governing.

Splendid is the merit of the heart in steady control, for with it one will be able to hear the 'sound of the single hand'. Without it, it is useless to talk about enlightenment or illusion. A man wearing a stole or priest's robe looks very fine, but if his heart is not in control, such apparel is merely funny. Without the controlling heart, it is useless to go on the pilgrims' rounds of the Western counties[60] and the four provinces.[61] The controlling heart is our elixir instrument, as good as the hermit's elixirs of old. This elixir needs no pots or pans.

Old lady heart-control, how old are you? I am the same age as the void. Old father-void may die or not, as he pleases, but I am always present. The mountains and rivers and the whole earth are my children, so I never lack anything.

For a warrior who has been reared by his lord's goodness, it is right to be cautious. Proper caution is the mark of a warrior who has placed his body at the disposal of his lord. It is still his own body, but he cannot be entirely free with it. He must keep it carefully. Even if he is called bad names, 'dog' and so on, he must not become angry. For when one is living on behalf of his lord, he cannot refuse to go to the bottom-most hell. As long as life lasts, he must cut through all his own private interests. This is the eternal abode of the brave warrior.

Old lady heart-control, where are you? I dwell in the elixir field and the sea of spirit. The merit of this elixir is so great that it can break into pieces and grind into powder the high Mount Sumeru and the very void itself. It makes all ten regions, all reality, all attachment, though visible — invisible. Life and death and nirvana itself, become yesterday's dream. Nor does it leave any trace of illusion or bodhi-wisdom. And there is now no hell into which one may fall, nor any paradise into which one may climb. But without this elixir of mine, one will have to perform hard works and undergo hard discipline for twenty or thirty long years, before one can attain to such a condition — unless one comes across the knowledge of true enlightenment.

Some there are who, though they have not reached this state, say they have, and think they can just follow the dictates of their own hearts. Murder, theft, such things they say, leave no mark upon the heart: 'The five obstructions and the ten evils are now quite a comfort, for we have left the law of karma behind.' Such are the words of self-will which comes from uninhibited false views. It is really terrible to contemplate such minds, for one knows that the very discernment which one has struggled to obtain, the sense *(dharma)* of discrimination becomes more than ever a seed producing hellish states. The original heart-control has melted away, and in its stead there are devilish effects, long-nosed goblins *(tengu)*[62] running around inside the mind. When people manage the laws of karma so foolishly — unless they happen to meet a clear-minded teacher — they will never be able to discover the mystery attained by enlightenment.

If what seems to be happening now continues in India, China, or in our own country, true Zen discipline will utterly fall to the ground and strange false dharmas will be established.

There are some who say that the Zen sects (Obaku, Soto, Rinzai) all provide true wisdom but that it is only necessary to listen to their teachings. 'It is not necessary,' they say, 'to practise their meditation, nor is it necessary to resort to their sutra or patriarchal records. Behind the divine avatars are the real buddhas, and if one searches for real buddhas one will be led astray. If one searches for the dharma, one may lose its real meaning. Buddhahood and bodhi-wisdom are but a dream. Life and death and nirvana, are but the track of a bird through the air. Do not bother about good and evil. Spend your months and days in the white land of the undistorted and real buddhas. If you disturb the waters of the stream, it will become muddy. Do not inquire, do not learn, do not put forth your hand.'

But if our law of meditation is true, the more important and valuable must it be for the crowd of foolish and lazy people of today. People do not realise that we are all living buddhas. They just eat and pass on, and when we see them sleeping side by side, we see them as people rowing side by side in a boat, and we wonder what sort of destination they will reach. Is this not an omen of the destruction of the dharma?

What, then, should be undertaken as the correct discipline of enlightenment? Perhaps old lady heart-control knows, so let us ask her.

The dharma has really been given up for the last five hundred years. A large number of people do not know anything about true wisdom, which, however, is the most important business for us. In ancient times there was a revelation about this from the great god of Kasuga. It was given to Kedatsu Shonin,[63] who was told that since the time of Kuruson Buddha (Krakucchanda, fourth of the seven Buddhas of the earlier eras of Buddhism), those who did not possess the heart-wisdom, no matter how wise they might have been in other ways, were but teachers of a false way.

And it is this heart-wisdom that the old lady sang about in the mountains. It is the wisdom which seeks enlightenment, not only for its own sake, but so that it may be able to pass on that wisdom to others. It puts the whip to the four vows of the Buddha, and makes people urgent in helping others. This is the most important part of the dharma. This dharma duty is above all other works. Oh, how beautiful and gracious it is. Even with a Buddha's mouth, its praises cannot be exhausted. It requires true discernment. But with discernment alone and no performance, our own breasts will provide but little nourishment. And with so little nourishment, it will not be possible to rear any children. If you cease after a successful search to attain to the music of the 'sound of one hand' and rest in that success alone, that is nothing better than the heretical teaching about there being no 'effects of karma'. In such a case, one would have to pass through the thousandfold depths of the jungle.

And old lady heart-control, when you die where will you go? Stop the sailing boat and be still. One's duty is not fulfilled until one has passed round the forty-nine bends[64] of the narrow mountain road. And what is the colour and scent of the wind there? The direct heart-to-heart teaching has been transmitted from Daruma to Eka (the second Chinese Zen Patriarch). In this there are the thousand sicknesses and obstacles which fill up the breasts of disciples. If there were none of these obstacles, Zen would die out.

One must risk one's life to break through these obstacle barriers, to open these locks. Without these, it would not be true Zen teaching. There must be difficulties even as there are difficulties for the carp which leaps up the ten thousand leagues of the Dragon's Way, and in the way of the fox which has to pass through the sacred Torii of the Inari goddess. Even if one's daily food is Zen, the duties and correct conditions are not fulfilled unless one breaks through these locks and barriers.

All the great teachers clearly perceived each thing, one by one, and searched the sutras through, and even studied outside teachings. That was the way in which they gathered innumerable treasures of the dharma. Only thus were they able to save the two powers[65] of hearing and obeying the dharma. It is inside these powers that we must seek for the 'seedling'. Be sure to find that seedling. The temples and Shinto protection are both required for this. They are like the two wings of a bird enabling it to fly. But the great work is that of the bodhisattvas, and this will persist, even if the great void were to end.

Do not be negligent. Keep your body in good health. With this last word, the old lady will bring her talk to a close.

The Calm Mind Beating Out the Dust

Anshin Hokori Tataki

Down, down. Prostrate yourselves before the Tathagata Shakyamuni. Hello, everybody. Listen! Listen to me, won't you?

People in every land recognise the authority of their own parents, but not so Siddhartha who was the Buddha.

From the days of his youth he became fond of going about the world, just as if he had been a merchant. He threw away the family rank which he had inherited. He threw it away with a 'pop'. And when he was nineteen[66] he went away into the mountains. There he begged two hermits, Alara and Kalara,[67] to be his teachers. For them he gathered the bark of trees, he drew water, he cut firewood. Thus he heaped up capital until at the end of thirty years he was able to open his own store. This store he called the Kegon Store (the *Mahavaipulya Buddhavatamsaka Sutra* teaching). Here he had a splendid stock of goods for sale. Soon after opening this store, two men came to buy. One was called Manjushri (Monju) and the other was Samantabhadra (Fugen). But the goods were too highly priced for most people, and the other customers seem to have been either blind or deaf. At any rate they would not look at his wares. As this would never do, he started off with another assortment and began to display cheaper goods. These he called *Agama*. No sooner had he switched on this message, than his shop began to be crowded with regular customers. So, little by little, he laid in a bigger stock of goods and widened out his business with the *Mahaprajnaparamita sutras*; and seizing the opportunity he skilfully sold to his clients the *Saddharma Pundarika Sutra* and the *Mahaparinirvana Sutra,* each according to his nature and qualifications. Then a famous man named Sudatta took a fancy to him and provided him with a mansion called the Jetavana Vihara where he could display his wares. From this time his fame began to spread and his business flourished. Everyone under heaven praised him and called him their father.

About this time one of his medicines, called the *Law of the Lotus*, the *Secret of the Wondrous Law*, became very popular. One of those who purchased this was the little daughter of Sagara, the Dragon King. She took the medicine and became as enlightened as the Buddha himself. But at this time also the unconquered King Ajatashatru (Ajase-o)[68] (son of Bimbisara) joined in a secret plot with Devadatta to close the store. In carrying out the plot this king imprisoned his mother, Vaidehi, so that she would not be able to purchase any of Shakyamuni's goods. The poor lady hated this world as a joyless land and suffered from an illness called the 'Sickness of the Five Obstacles' for women, as well as from the three obediences (obstacles to woman's salvation). Realising that she had no spiritual capital, she prayed that if there were any medicine to meet her case, it might be sent to her.

When one prays to Shakyamuni even from a great distance, he is aware of it. He perceived that there might be many customers like this lady, so he began to sell some goods which he had stored away in his warehouse for more than forty years. Then with two assistants, Ananda and Maudgalyayana, he went to the king's palace and gave Vaidehi a tasteful medicine, a medicine which he had compounded at the time he took his great vow during the five kalpas. This medicine is the 'calling upon the name of Amida', and it is wrapped up in the six syllables *'na-mu-a-mi-da-butsu'*. It means absolute concentration on Amida's name. It makes no difference whether this is taken before or after birth in this world.

For this medicine, no capital or special wisdom is needed. All one has to do is recite the words with one's mouth. The thoughts of the mind may perhaps be unsettled — not yet having attained to the stage of the wisdom of the heavenly eye — and the wisdom may be so feeble that it will never be a capital wisdom. Shakyamuni warned people that for such a serious trouble as that of the five obstacles,[69] for which hope has been given up, there is no other medicine. In the case of this lady herself and her five hundred attendants, all the doctors of the three worlds had thrown up the sponge, because it was now a chronic disease due to wrongful actions performed before the beginning of the age, and to illusions and doubts in a sick mind. But here was this marvellous medicine on the spot and at the instant — just by repetition of the mystic word *'ano-kutara'*[70] which healed whilst the sweat poured out of the body. Here indeed is a pivot of fundamental power.

Do I hear you say: 'Too easy! Such wares are intended to deceive only old men and women?' Many doubt their efficacy and ask of the wise if there is not some other way more suited for clever people. And Shakyamuni pointed straight back at the heart of man and said that, within one's own heart, there is to be found the true buddha-nature. Then the Buddha smiled. So also did Mahakashyapa who received these particular kinds of goods. These goods are the main truths which have been handed down in succession from one generation of disciples to another.

Open your eyes and look! What is Shakyamuni? And what are we? We shall see the inexpressible mind-nature, enlightened and complete calm, seeing nothing, doing nothing. We shall have unearthed a marvellous treasure. When you begin to practise meditation — seeing with the real eyes — at first you may become drowsy. Your knees may tremble. Your back may hurt. The pupils of your eyes may dilate. This is when you must persevere. Rouse yourself! You will feel like that time when something you lent your neighbour three years ago, was unexpectedly returned. 'Three pints of black beans, one bushel of chaff.' Utter illusion when you recall these to your mind.

But if that particular method does not suit your nature, are there any other goods hawked round in this trade? What about the secret mystery of Shingon? Here we come across that mystic syllable 'A' which represents the first principle — the principle of negation — of the non-birth of the elements of existence. This principle must become a sort of endowment within one's own mind. Next there is the mystic syllable 'Ra'[71] which represents the elements *(dharmas)* within each individual mind, and which discriminates sense objects and discerns the five wisdoms,[72] the five fundaments as well as the diamond and womb realms. All these objects of our sense-knowledge are born within our breasts, as if we were their parents. When we know this we rise to the rank of buddha. These goods are goods in the trade of self-salvation.

But although this is a quick and perfect way of becoming a Buddha, as taught in the Law of the Lotus, and is an excellent medicine, yet we do not all have the patience needed for it. So it is no better than an advertisement sign pointing to the opening words of the sutras. Even if we proceed to read them we do not have the capital wisdom sufficient to purchase these goods, so we turn to the truth which was not revealed for forty years, and this is the six syllable name,[73] which is an abbreviation of the *Lotus Sutra (Saddharma Pundarika)*. When you have swallowed this medicine, which is the eight rolls of these unexcelled scriptures, then you will be born into the western paradise of Amida.

Which of all these goods will you choose? It is a matter of calculating. Rather than taking the long way round, would you not choose the short route, which needs no money or toll, but just requires you to call on the name of Amida? It may be wise to choose to wear coarse clothes, to eat only twice a day and to practise the discipline according to the rules, but it will be useless unless we 'catch either the fleas or the lice'. Even if you do not actually put out your hand to steal, if you covet a thing in your heart, that is the parent of evil. When there is no mother, there will be no child. And also 'everybody tells a lie sometimes'. What about our behaviour at weddings and such events, even if we do not get drunk? One cannot pass through life without the ten thousand intercourses. No wonder we cannot observe the five rules. Whatever you may think about these methods of the Buddha's trade, none of them can be carried out without patience and perseverance. So, whatever you do, come back to the Buddha's teaching, and carry on that trade which needs no capital wisdom, i.e. the six syllabled name. That will require all your patience. But if you have some capital wisdom to spend, try the self-relying method. If your capital is too slim, however, that will not do, for when your fortune has all been spent, you will go astray and find yourself stranded in a field of tea-shrubs.

So listen to the old story. The great founders of the sects all had plenty of capital wisdom, yet they did not despise or reject this good medicine of the six syllables. Much more then, should not we who have no wisdom capital and little patience, decide not to hobble along on a self-relying way, but rather ride in the boat of that method which tells us to rely on the other?

An ordinary mortal can become a Buddha! This is like a tile or a stone becoming gold! If you think I am telling lies, then go and ask the priest at your temple. Oh, everybody, how happy should we be. Confucianism and Shintoism are rival tradesmen. They call our teaching by all sorts of bad names, but the Buddha's is a store of long established business and it is really marvellous. Its original office was in a side street in India, but it established a branch office in our land. Now its wares are on sale in all the eight and nine sects. If one does not like these goods, there is nowhere else to go for them. So with all respect I urge everybody of all ranks to make use of this tablet medicine of the six syllables every morning and night. Then the four seas will be calm; the present age will be prosperous; the next generations will be long-lived. The prayers of this age and the blessings of the next age will not produce anything better than these.

I am not telling lies. Shakyamuni has not made a muddle of things. This is the real dharma.

Dated, the tenth month of the first year in the sign of the Monkey, in the era of Meiwa (1764), under the Sal tree. Spoken by the aged Sendai.

Songs in Praise of Meditation

Zazen Wasan[74]

The primary essence of all sentient beings is buddha.
The originating nature of the self is the
   non-buddha-nature.
Without sentient beings there is no buddha.

The reckless way of utter absorption is the true way,
As one who is immersed in water.
So make the thought of the non-thought the whole
   of your thought.

Even when one is tramping along dark roads,
Those roads are themselves the Lotus Land.
This is more than sufficient for rejoicing and praise.

Even as water and ice go together,
So good works of graciousness
Do not know any attachment to sentient things.
Nevertheless, they destroy the innumerable
   accumulations of sins.
They are like the utterance of the mystic cry
   (at enlightenment).

How thankworthy is the dharma.
By it the causes and relationships of the six regions
    of the Wheel
Receive endless happiness.
Escape from the life-death cycle will take place.

Almsgiving, obedience to the dharma, the *paramitas* —
All are but the dark road of our own ignorance.
But all of them come to an end in the dharma.
As for the meditation of the Mahayana,
Where can the evil regions be?

Recollection of the Buddha, repentance,
    the discipline of life —
When once these have entered our ears,
Then he who performs one meritorious act
    of meditation
Much more he who has 'turned himself round'
From such the Pure Land is not far distant.

He who has ceased from vain argumentation,
He who extols and rejoices in the goodness of others,
He who realises that 'form' is 'non-form',
He who bears witness to the nature of the self
    as originating essence.

To such an one, singing and dancing are alike
    the voice of the dharma,
He has opened the gate of the absolute
    undifferentiated nature.
When that happens, what is there to seek?

Whether one goes on or returns, there is no
  'elsewhere'.
The very body he has is, indeed, Buddha.

The sky of the unhindered *samadhi* is broad
Just as there can be no ice without water,
  so nirvana is immediately present.
To go seeking it in distant places — how foolish —
So do you become the son of that rich man.

Endnotes

1. Introspection: The practice of looking for truth in one's own mind, in contrast to the study of the outward universe and objective phenomena. The calming of the mind and the contemplation of it.

2 Four Great Vows are taken by bodhisattvas to accomplish the task which they have undertaken. Amitabha (Amida) made forty-eight vows. Shakyamuni has five hundred vows attributed to him. Various interpretations are given:

> (i) To nourish perpetually the minds which are seeking the Way — this is like the Great Earth.
> (ii) To ferry all sentient beings over to nirvana — this is like a great boat.
> (iii) To moisten and soak all sentient beings in the delicious taste of the dharma — this is like a great sea.
> (iv) To include all sentient beings within the scope of the task, and testify to them concerning the buddha-nature — this is like the great sky.

> OR:
> (i) To ferry across all who have not yet crossed to the other shore.
> (ii) To explain the dharma to those who do not yet understand.
> (iii) To give peace to those who have not yet found it.
> (iv) To make those who have not yet reached it, attain to nirvana.

> OR:
> (i) To know the immeasurable buddha-body and teach this truth to all sentient beings (called the *Muhen Seigwan Ho*).
> (ii) To cut away all illusions and ignorance, separate all life-death relationship from the world and from all the sentient beings in the six regions (called the *Honno Muso Seigwan*).
> (iii) To discover all the inexhaustible entrances into the dharma and teach them to sentient beings (called the *Homon Mujin Seigwan Ho*).
> (iv) To bear witness to the unexcelled nature of buddhahood (called the *Butsu Mujo Seigwan Ho*).

(Here it may be interesting to point out at least one of the results of Hakuin's resolve to perform the Great Vows. The *Yasen Kanna* is the most widely read of Hakuin's books. It is said that most of its readers were sufferers from consumption. This was then believed to be absolutely incurable, and sufferers were filled with despair. But in this book Hakuin told how he himself 'emaciated by the disease and in utter despair' had been able to cure himself, and had lived on into his eighties. Many said they had 'been saved just by hearing the title of this book'!

Hakuin not only personally tasted the joy of recovery but took the vow to help similar sufferers in his own age and in the ages after him. And that is why he wrote this book.

It is not only in matters of physical health that Hakuin's strength of character is seen to be based on his religious vows.

Little reference is made in Hakuin's works to his artistic interests. Perhaps one reason for this may be found in the following account of a visit he once paid to a rich man in the town of Matsuyama.

The host had invited several monks to a dinner, and after the feast, had entertained them by showing them various pictures and samples of calligraphy, which the host valued highly for their intrinsic merit. Amongst these pictures was a painting by a priest called Dai-gu. There was, Hakuin thought, a certain lack of force in this picture which made it difficult for him to praise its artistic merit. Yet the owner seemed to esteem this as his greatest treasure. This made Hakuin think within himself that if such a carelessly painted picture could be so highly valued, it must be because of the moral integrity of the artist rather than in any artistic skill. It followed, thought Hakuin, that the skill or otherwise of the artist was of little importance or value in itself. So when he returned to his own home he immediately threw all his art and calligraphy books, brushes, inks and pictures into the fire, and began to devote himself entirely to the essentials of religion. Art seems to have become quite secondary to him. (Fortunately, not all his paintings and calligraphy were thus destroyed.)

3 The Thirty-seven Ablutions *(saikai)*, means the abstinence from food, and cleansing the body, i.e. being careful about the control of the mind and body.

4 A Thousand Deaths: This is described in detail in the Sho Shikwan *(Hsiao chih-kuan). [T'ien-tai hsiao chih-kuan,* see Carl Bielefeldt's

discussion of this point in his *Dogen's Manuals of Zen Meditation* 1988 pp. 71-72.]

5 Seven Verticals (and the Eight Horizontals): The vertical energy of the Buddha which operates directly, as it were, from above down to the mind of sentient beings who are thus enlightened by 'quick' and direct power. This is the Way of 'self-reliance', the Way which sees the truth within the mind itself without any external aid from teachers or sutras, and needs no accommodated truth. The horizontal energy of the Buddha, on the other hand, spreads throughout the universe, as it were, and reaches all sentient beings (those who rely on the strength of others, e.g. Amida, and those who are helped by accommodated truth). The numbers 'seven' and 'eight' refer to the number of sects in each kind of teaching.

6 Hei: The ideogram for day used here is the day when the mystic leaf of the herb Hei falls off. The herb is Shepherd's Purse. It was believed to produce one leaf each day for the first fifteen days of the month, and then to shed one leaf each day for the last fifteen days. This was an old tradition coming down from the times of the first dynasty in China. The twenty-fifth day refers to the writer's old age, approaching the very end.

7 *Orate Gama:* This strange name is said to have been chosen by Hakuin for this book because he always used to have in front of him a little kettle or pot for brewing tea whilst he was writing. One story is that he used what may perhaps be called a sort of slang *'Ora'* for 'my' and *'Te'* for 'hand' and then the word 'kettle' — simply meaning 'my kettle'. Another suggestion is that the ideograms for O-Ra-Te were embossed on the kettle *(gama)*.

8 Darkness and Scattering: *'Kon'* is used of the darkness which comes after death. It signifies the darkness of unenlightenment, in contrast to *'san',* which signifies the 'scattering' of the *skandhas* or elements of existence when enlightenment is attained.

9 Special Services and ceremonies in which the priests march in procession round the Buddha-seat from right to left, intoning the scriptures.

10 Reality of Self: The ideograms *'ji-sho'* mean 'self' and 'nature'. Jisho is activated by the spiritual entity whereby all the differentiated phenomena of the universe appear.

11 Three Realities Within the Universe: The reality called the 'void', the

reality called the 'temporary reality', and the 'middle' reality — the inner. These three realities are connected with the activity of meditation. 'Void meditation' is self-explanatory. 'Temporary reality meditation' is when one perceives no actual reality, but sees that there is an obvious distinction of form or colour. 'Inner reality meditation' is when one perceives that the elements neither exist nor non-exist; they are at the same time void and existent, the absolute, the phenomenal and the assumed realities.

12 Wheel of Life: This consists of six regions or realms in which sentient beings might find themselves as a result of their own actions. The six regions are: (i) the hell realm, (ii) the realm of the pretas or hungry ghosts, (iii) the animal realm, (iv) the realm of fierce demons or jealous gods who fight against the dharma, (v) the human realm, (vi) and the deva realm, the land of the gods, the heavenly realm.

13 Yura: The priest Ippen is said to have 'handed on the lamp of the dharma' *(Ten-Do)*. He belonged to a sub-sect of Zen called the 'Ho-To-Ha Lamp of the Dharma'; it is also called the 'Yura Monto' sect. It was founded by a priest named Emmyo Kokushi who lived at Yura.

14 Sudden Ignorance: This is one of the three hindrances: (i) Error concerning the four noble truths, (ii) ignorance concerning affairs and phenomena, and (iii) ignorance. This is the exact opposite of the state of genuine enlightenment. It is the activity of the mind which creates or produces all illusionary phenomena. It is the state of being unrelated to the absolute.

15 The Four Virtues are attained by listening to the dharma: (i) The great wisdom produced by hearing the true dharma, (ii) discerning the emptiness of reasoning concerning the four noble truths, (iii) separation from all hindrances or delusions, (iv) destruction of delusion and attainment of nirvana.

16 Cintamani Jewel: One of the seven jewels. The *mani* jewel is always clean and bright and shedding forth light. It is a symbol of the Buddha and his teaching *(cp. Om Mani Padme Hum)*. It can produce wonderful treasures according to the will of whoever possesses it. It is held in the hands of the two-handed goddess of compassion. It is kept safe in the palace of Makara, the dragon king, under the sea. It is said to proceed out of the brain of this dragon king. It is the jewel which is used by Taishakuten (Indra) in his battle with the demons.

17 Bright Light: The light which shines from the mind and body of the Buddha and Bodhisattvas. It is the appearance of wisdom. It brightly illuminates all the common elements and all the teachings. It shines in all the ten regions of the universe, breaking down illusions and ignorance. It has two aspects or 'rays': the 'mind-light', and the 'colour or form-light' (called 'the body-light'). The latter has a constant glow and also a 'free-shining flashing light' which shines in the present rather than in the past.

18 Wisdom Eye: The wisdom eye sees that all dharmas are in reality void. By means of this eye, the *shravakas* or beginners cease from attachment to the differentiations of the phenomenal universe. It is one of the 'five eyes': the eye of the flesh, the eye of heaven, the eye of dharma, the eye of wisdom, and the eye of the Buddha.

19 Six-sided Temple: This is said to have been built by Shotoku Daishi. It contains the mausoleum of Tada Manju.

20 Five Schools of Thought: According to the Kegon sect the first generation of the Buddha's teachings separated — beginning with the 'shallow' and advancing to the 'deep'. This is the explanation of the term Go-Ha (five sects) given by Ho Zo, the founder of the Kegon sect (642-712) which is based on the *Mahavaipulya Buddhavatamsaka Sutra*. The five sects given are: (i) Hinayana; (ii) the beginning teachings of the Mahayana; (iii) the end teachings of the Mahayana *(Lokavantara Sutra)*; (iv) the sudden teaching of the Mahayana; and (v) the Kegon teaching itself.

21 Seven Currents of Illusion: The currents that carry away sentient beings by the sea of illusion. The methods for bringing these currents to an end are: (i) Causing desire to cease; (ii) causing delusions of thought to cease; (iii) the perception of the four noble truths; (iv) the perception of the emptiness of all the dharmas of existence; (v) the perception that the mind is 'void'; (vi) the protection from any recurrence of the habit of sense or thought; (vii) the final prevention of any such recurrence.

22 Mount Sumeru: This is regarded as the central mountain of every universe. It rises out of the ocean. Its sides are of gold, silver, lapis lazuli and crystal. It is also covered with fragrant shrubs.

23 Eight Upsets: These are the views which upset correct reasoning, and the views still believed in by *shravakas* and *pratyekabuddhas*. The first four are held by ordinary householders: The view that inconstant things

are constant, that non-pleasure is pleasure, that what is non-self is self, that impure things are pure. The second set of four are held by monks of the two lower orders: That the constant reality of nirvana is not constant, that pleasure is not pleasure, that the self is non-self, that purity is not purity.

24 Eight Voices of the Buddha: Pleasant, fear-producing, respectful, compassionate, sincere, deep, soft, and inexhaustible.

25 The Sal Tree *(Shorea Robusta)* is called firm, hard and victorious because it grows tall and overshadows other trees in the forest. Shakyamuni's conception and birth took place under a sal tree.

26 Pilgrim Way. The term is used of travelling monks. By regulation, a monk when travelling must use a 'pilgrim's staff' so the word *'hishaku'* or 'staff' came to be used of a travelling Buddhist monk.

27 Three Ages. These are the three innumerable ages, the time it takes for a bodhisattva to study and meditate prior to reaching buddhahood or nirvana.

28 Dharani: These are magic formulas which prevent good dharmas or elements from being lost, prevent the duties of infinity from being scattered, and which take away the evil dharmas from sentient beings and provide them with good dharmas. It is a name which is also used for titles and for scriptures which provide such merits for sentient beings. In the *Yogacarya Sutra* four kinds of *dharani* are named. In the *Mahaprajnaparamita Sutra* three kinds are named.

29 Three Mysteries: One mystery is seen in the very nature of the body, one in the word, and one by the mind. Alternatively, one is of the hands, one of the mouth, and one of the will. Or, again, one is the mystery of the Buddha, one is that of will, and one of the bodhisattva.

30 Three Sutras: The three sections of the *Saddharma Pundarika (Muryogi-kyo, Hokke-kyo* and *Kwan Buken-kyo),* or the three sections of the *Vairocana* sutras, or the three Pure Land sutras, or the three sections of the scriptures concerning the defence of the country *(Chin-gokoku-ron).*

31 Five Sacred Books. The sacred books used by the Ritsu sect: (i) Binimo-kyo, (ii) Zenken-ron, (iii) Myoryo-ron, (iv) Mu-toku-koku-ka-ron, and (v) Sabbata-ron.

32 Seven Sects: Risshu, Hossoshu, Sanronshu, Kegonshu, Tendaishu, Shingonshu, and Zenshu.

33 Seven Treasures: Gold, silver, emerald, pearl, crystal, ruby and agate.

34 The Ten Worlds of Illusion and Enlightenment: The hell state, the realm of the hungry ghosts, the animal realm, the realm of the jealous gods *(asuras)*, the heavenly realm, and the human realm (the six realms of illusion). Then the *shramanas, pratyekabuddhas, bodhisattvas* and *buddhas* are the four realms of enlightenment.

35 The Secret or Mystic teachings: The secret is the teaching given by the Buddha through his mystic or magic powers. The crowds who were listening heard but one sound of his voice, but it meant something different to each listener according to that person's capacity to understand.

36 Non-originated: That which is not the effect of any cause. That which is constant, not created by any dharma. Its opposite is UI, the phenomenal world.

37 Great Mirror: When all mental activities up from ignorance are brushed away, is anything left? The mental activities are likened to dust which has settled on a mirror. They are the 'six dusts', or the 'ten sleeps', or the 'five heretical opinions', or the 'five aggregations of dharma elements'. They conceal the surface of the mirror. When wiped off, true wisdom is seen. This real wisdom perceives the dharma elements for what they are. Just as all objects are reflected in a mirror, so all the dharmas are reflected in this 'mirror-wisdom', which is the first wisdom attained on enlightenment. Therefore, this wisdom is called the 'great round or perfect mirror'. When this mirror is looked into, what is seen cannot be expressed in words, explained by teachers, written in sutras or shown as symbols.

38 Pure Land of Calm and Light: The universe as seen by those who have awakened, those for whom this universe is a pure land where there is no defilement, where all differences are harmonised, and where eternal calm is united with wisdom and benevolence. In other words, it is the universe as seen by the Buddha.

39 The Five Ranks are mentioned in the *Hoshi* section of the *Lotus Sutra:* (i) Those who receive and memorise the dharma *(Juji Hoshi)*, (ii) those who see and read the dharma or sutra *(Dokkyo Hoshi)*, (iii) those who do not see but repeat the sutra by heart *(Tsukyo Hoshi)*, (iv) those who expound the sacred text *(Kaisetsu Hoshi)*, (v) those who copy out the sutra *(Shosha Hoshi)*.

40 Smile — The Plucked Flower Smile: The legend is that Shakyamuni whilst on the Vulture Peak, received a red flower from Brahma and used it instead of giving a dharma talk. Only Mahakashyapa understood. This is the original story of the *'Shoho Ganzo Nehan Nyoshi'* or *Direct Dharma of Vision [Shobogenzo, True Dharma Eye]* — the wonder-heart of the Buddha coming directly from heart-to-heart without words.

41 Five Duties of Life: Almsgiving, obedience to the rules, patience, ascetic practice, meditation. Alternatively, the five works of bodhisattvas: obedience to the rules, meditation, wisdom, saving others, and sympathy with the sick.

42 Embudangon: The Japanese name for the river full of golden sand which flows under the jambu (embu) tree. The land through which this river flows is the continent where there are less pleasures to be enjoyed than in the other two continents of the Buddhist universe, but this (Jambu) continent surpasses the others in real joy because it is here only that one may meet the Buddha and listen to him.

43 Non-self: We might have the idea of a real 'ego', but there is no place in our bodies for such a controlling principle. There is no precise real self by any combination of the *skandhas*, nor is there any controlling principle apart from or unconnected with the *skandhas*. Moreover, even the dharmas are not real existences in themselves, i.e. there is no real existence of phenomena, nor of feelings. All these are but combinations of *skandhas*. And they do not exist apart from the *skandhas*.

44 Non-attachment: The condition of being entirely separated from all attachment to things, having no more fondness or desire for them. The condition of knowing that all things are but phantasms or illusions. The term is also used for those bodhisattvas who perceive the void with their hearts whilst still in the world of the non-absolute.

45 Stopping: Entry into the calm of nirvana where for the first time real happiness is found.

46 The Seven Buddhas of whom six were forerunners of Shakyamuni: Vipashyin, Shikhin, Vishvabhu (these three were Buddhas of the previous kalpa era), Krakucchanda, Kanakamuni, Kashyapa and Shakyamuni (these four are of the present kalpa era.

47 I Ro Ha Ni Ho He To: This syllabary is a poem, attributed to Kobo Daishi, roughly translated as:

Though 'colour' may be fragrant,
It scatters and is dispersed.
This world of ours
Is impermanent in everyone's case.
We cross the distant mountains today
And see nothing but a shallow dream,
But we do not become inebriated with it.

48 Eight Falsities: False ideas concerning life, destruction, the past, the future, the one, variety or change, the bringing to an end, and permanence.

49 Ten Rules *(ju-zen-kai)* for Novices: Kill not, steal not, tell no lies, commit no fornication, do not speak falsely, do not use abusive language, do not flatter, do not be avaricious, do not be wrathful, do not hold false views.

50 Five Rules for Laypeople: Not to kill, steal, commit fornication, speak recklessly, drink intoxicating liquors.

51 Purifying the Six Roots: Cutting off attachment to the six senses and arriving at the 800 merits of sight, the 1,200 merits of hearing, the 800 merits of the sense of smell, the 1,200 merits of the mouth, the 800 merits of the body, and the 1,200 merits of the mind activities.

52 Five Human Relationships: Parent and child, lord and retainer, husband and wife, brothers, and friends.

53 Five Eternal Virtues: Benevolence, righteousness, propriety, fidelity, wisdom.

54 Henjaku: The name of a famous Chinese physician who lived in the fourth century AD.

55 Kiba: An illegitimate son of King Bimbisara who gave up his claim to succeed to the throne in order to practise medicine. He lived in the sixth century BC, and is said to have cured Shakyamuni from an illness. He converted and brought to repentance Ajatashatru (Ajase-o) who had killed his own father.

56 Torii of Inari: A torii is a traditional Japanese gate most commonly found at the entrance of or within Shinto shrines, which symbolically marks the transition from the mundane to the sacred. The Fushimi Inari shrine is the most important of several thousands of shrines dedicated to Inari, the Shinto god of rice. Foxes are thought to be Inari's messengers,

resulting in many fox statues across the shrine grounds. Situated in Kyoto, this particular shrine consists of thousands of vermillion torii gates which straddle a network of trails behind its main buildings.

57 'Namu' means 'veneration, praise, hail, or adoration'; it is the sacred word at the beginning of such formulas as *'namu Amida Butsu'* or *'namu myo ho renge kyo'*.

58 Nyozegamon ('Thus Have I Heard'). These are the opening words that occur at the beginning of all the sutras of the Buddhas of past eras. 'Thus' is the accompaniment of faith; 'I heard' is the accompaniment of hearing. Ananda announced that he had thus heard the teaching of the Buddha. In this way, he assured his listeners of the authenticity of the sutras. The phrase is therefore the 'introductory evidence of faith'.

59 Mala Beads are often used at times of concentrating on the bodhisattvas and buddhas, or for counting the number of recitations of the 'nembutsu' formulas, etc.

60 Pilgrims' rounds of the Western counties: The pilgrimage to the thirty-three shrines of Kannon, where each image has special features, e.g. a thousand hands, or eleven faces, or is holding the sacred jewel, etc.

61 Pilgrims' Rounds of the Four Provinces: The pilgrimage to the eighty-eight shrines on the island of Shikoku, which are connected with Kobo Daishi.

62 Tengu: Various meanings are attached to this word: (i) The name of a constellation; (ii) light and darkness: *'ten'* (heaven) symbolising bright light *(kwomyo)*, meaning the enlightenment which is the fruit of buddhahood, and *'gu'* the darkness of folly, or the result of existence as a sentient being. Or (iii) *'ten'* (heaven) is combined with *mandara* and *'gu'* with *'chi'* (earth) *mandara*, implying the Diamond Realm and the Womb Realm (the Shingon School symbolic usage). (iv) Any followers of Enma, the king of hell. In the *Nihongi*, the ideogram *'gu'* is interpreted as *'kitsune'* (fox) and the word *'tengu'* is read as 'heavenly fox' *(ama-kitsune)*. This is a mythical animal supposed to live in the mountains, eating snakes, and has a body like a badger with a white head; or nowadays it is represented as a mystical mythical creature with human form and ghost-like, speaking strange oracles, and with a long nose and wings with which it is always flying about.

63 Kedatsu Shonin: There were two priests of this name: (i) Jokyo (1155-1213), the son of Fujiwara Shokei, a priest of the Hosso-shu famous as a teacher, and (ii) Ryozen (1048-1139) a Shingon priest who built many temples.

64 The Forty-nine Bends: The forty-nine days immediately after death, when special requiem ceremonies were performed at the temple of the deceased.

65 Two Powers: *'Kon'* is the power of becoming, the 'root' of things, and *'ki'* is the activity. *'Konki'*, therefore, means the power actively to practise the discipline after hearing the dharma.

66 Siddhartha Leaves Home: It is generally accepted in the Buddhist world that Siddhartha left home at the age of 29, not 19. However, as this chapter is clearly a parody, it should be taken in the spirit in which it is meant.

67 Alara Kalara for Alara Karan, signifying Alara Kalama. Alara was a hermit who lived near Vaishali. When Shakyamuni left Bhagava, he went to this hermit for instruction. In later times the one man was believed to be two, Alara and Kalara.

68 Ajatashatru (Ajase-o) (c. 500 BC) was the son of King Bimbisara of Magadha). Egged on by Devadatta, Ajatashatru killed his father and seized power over central India. Later, he converted to Buddhism and became a king of almsgiving. He was patron of the first Great Council and died twenty-four years after Shakyamuni. Vaidehi was his mother. She was imprisoned by him in the 'sevenfold' prison where she became so disenamoured of the world that she asked Shakyamuni to teach her from his Vulture Peak. The Buddha went from his assembly on that mountain and in her prison discoursed to her, thus producing the *Amitayurdhyana Sutra (Muryoju-kyo)*.

In this sutra, the lady Vaidehi asked the Buddha: 'Please teach me *Shiyui*, please teach me *Shoju.*' These two terms are of frequent occurrence in Hakuin's and other Zen works. *'Shiyui'* is the first part of the 'accommodation' teaching about meditation. It signifies the bringing into one's mind thoughts of sublimity about the pure land. *'Shoju'* is the real (not accommodated) meditation, in which thoughts become clearer and more detached, so that all relative and learned imagination is put to rest and the meditating mind alone remains. All the objects of sense are harmonised and made to correspond with *samadhi* until the Pure Land is seen in all its purity. In the Shinshu School, *'Shiyui'* is entry into faith by the gate of 'self-power' or reliance, whilst *'Shoju'* is the true mind of the diamond unbreakable vow of Amida — reliance upon Amida's power.

69 Five Obstacles: Hindrances to faith (doubt), progress (laziness), thought (anger), meditation (envy), and wisdom (ignorance and anger).

70 *Anokutara* is the abbreviation for *anuttara-samyak-sambodhi*, a phrase used as a name for Buddha's perfected, universal, supreme wisdom.

71 Ra: One of the fifty Sanskrit sounds. It represents the individual separate dharmas — the 'dust'. It is said to be the tone of voice of joy and victory over 'non-joy'.

72 Five Wisdoms: *Chi*, or wisdom activity of the mind, which discriminates between right and wrong, and good and evil. Sometimes it is classified in two divisions: *(ni-chi)*, wisdom which perceives reality, and wisdom which perceives phenomena. Sometimes it is in three divisions: the wisdom of the ordinary 'world liver', the wisdom of those who leave the world, and the wisdom of bodhisattvas and buddhas. The five wisdoms are those which are connected with the operation (or 'turning') of the 'nine sense-consciousnesses': (i) Wisdom which discerns the real nature of the dharmas *(hokai-no-taisho-chi)*; (ii) the discerning of all phenomena, as if reflected in a mirror *(daienkyo-chi)* (this wisdom is controlled by the Buddha Ashiku); (iii) the discernment of the identity (or equality) of 'this and that', non-discriminating wisdom *(byodo-sho-chi)* (Hosho is the Buddha who controls this wisdom); (iv) the discernment which cuts away doubts as to the dharma, and which distinguishes between true and false teaching *(myo-kansatsu-chi)*. This comes by turning away from the six sense-consciousnesses and by perceiving the 'self-nature' united with the nature of the dharma. Those who understand the working of the law of karma obtain this wisdom. Such persons are called *'Kendo'*, seers of the Way (Amida controls this wisdom); (v) the discernment which, having attained to buddhahood, turns away from the five sense-consciousnesses and, in order to bring joyful benefits to all sentient beings, teaches the various accommodated truths, as well as the ultimate truth. Fukujoju is the Buddha who controls this wisdom.

These five wisdoms are distributed or 'married' to the six 'great fundaments' which compose the body (earth, fire, etc., and consciousness itself), of which the first five belong to the Womb Realm and the sixth belongs to the Diamond Realm. They are also 'married' to the five Buddhas mentioned above. Vairocana is the centre of the Diamond. The others (Akshobhya, Ratnasambhava, Amoghasiddhi, and Amitabha) belong to the Womb Realm.

The five wisdoms are also interpreted as: (i) Wisdom of ordinary mortals; (ii) wisdom of *shravakas* (beginners); (iii) wisdom of *pratyekabuddhas*; (iv) wisdom of bodhisattvas; (v) wisdom of buddhas. There are also five degrees of buddha-wisdom: (i) Wisdom in general; (ii) wonderful wisdom; (iii) inexpressible wisdom; (iv) great-vehicle wisdom; and (v) incomparable wisdom.

73 The Six Syllable Name is *Na-mu-A-mi-da-Butsu*. It occurs in the *Amitayurdhyana* Sutra and is the name of Amida called upon for salvation.

74 Wasan: Poems composed in the Japanese language in praise of the Buddha: (i) For the purpose of explaining the scriptures to those who are entirely ignorant of them, and (ii) for singing or chanting by groups of devotees. The best known of these are by Genshin (942-1017), a Tendai priest, whose title was Eshin Soza, and by Senkwan (918-983), whose Wasan were in praise of Amida's Pure Land. Shinran (1173-1262), the founder of the Shinshu School, composed his Wasan when he was seventy-six years of age. Some of his poems were in praise of the patriarchs from Nagarjuna to Genku (117 poems), and some are known as the *Shozomatsu Wasan,* which Shinran composed when he was eighty-six, after having a dream or vision. These were in praise of Amida and Shakyamuni for producing faith in us mortals.

Index

Bibliography

Edkins, J., *Chinese Buddhism*. London. Kegan Paul, Trench Trubner & Co., 1899.

Eitel, E. J., *Handbook for the Student of Chinese Buddhism*, Japan, Lane Crawford & Co., 1870.

Eliot, Sir Charles, *Japanese Buddhism*, London, Routledge, Kegan Paul, 1959.

Inouye, Shuten, *Hekiganroku Shi Kowa*, Tokyo, Kyobunsha, 1934.

Ed. Kawamura, *Taitaro, Bukkyo Kakushu Koyo*, Tokyo, Kaiba Shoin, 1901.

Kimura, Shuzo, *Hakuin Zenji to sono Goroku*, Tokyo, Tamura Hajime, 1928.

Murakami, Sensho, *Nippon Bukkyo Shiko*, Tokyo, Kinkodo Shoseki Kabushiki Kwaisha, 1898.

Murdoch, James, *History of Japan*, The Asiatic Society of Japan.

Sansom, G. B., *Japan*, New York, New Century Co., 1931.

Ed. Sasaki, Gessho, *Bukkyo Jiten, Tokyo*, Muga Sambo, 1909.

Suzuki, Daisetz, *Manual of Zen Buddhism*, Eastern Buddhist Society, 1935.

Suzuki, Shujiro, *Hakuin Hogo Shu*, Tokyo, Sankyo Shoin, 1935.

Bibliography to 2021 edition

Yampolsky, Philip B., *The Zen Master Hakuin: Selected Writings*, Columbia University Press 1971.

Leggett, Trevor, *The Tiger's Cave: Translations of Japanese Zen Texts*, Routledge & Kegan Paul, 1977.

Waddell, Norman, *Wild Ivy: The Spiritual Autobiography of Zen Master Hakuin*, Shambhala Publications, Inc. 1999.

The *Soka Gakkai Dictionary of Buddhism*, 2002.

Also available from

Buddhist Publishing Group

Don't Take Your Life Personally
by Ajahn Sumedho

Ajahn Sumedho, an American Buddhist monk, urges us to trust in awareness and find out for ourselves what it is to experience genuine liberation from mental anguish and suffering. He encourages us not to take our lives personally, but to look at the reality of this moment free from beliefs, views and opinions; and he refers frequently to his own experiences along the path.

ISBN 9780946672318, 2010, paperback, 420 pages, and Kindle.

Zen Teaching of Instantaneous Awakening
by Zen Master Hui Hai,

translated by John Blofeld,

foreword by Charles Luk

Hui Hai was a great Zen Master of the same spiritual tradition as Hui Neng, Ma Tsu and Huang Po. His teaching touched this precise moment of truth.

> When things happen, make no response:
> keep your minds from dwelling on anything whatsoever:
> keep them for ever still as the void and utterly pure (without stain):

and thereby spontaneously attain deliverance.

(Hui Hai)

John Blofeld, a noted Buddhist author and translator, was one of the very few Englishmen to have experienced life in Chinese Buddhist temples and monasteries at first hand before the Communist revolution.

ISBN 9780946672035, 1962, 2007, paperback, 188 pages, and Kindle.

Experience Beyond Thinking
by Diana St Ruth

An easy to follow guide to Buddhist meditation and the reflections of an ordinary practitioner.

> Meditation allows us to see ourselves plainly as we are, as if standing before a large clear mirror. Nothing is hidden. It is like waking up from a dream into a new way of life completely free of all self-imposed restrictions and conflicting states of mind.

(Diana St Ruth)

ISBN 9780946672264, 1993, 2008, paperback, 172 pages.

Teachings of a Buddhist Monk
by Ajahn Sumedho

> Ajahn Sumedho invites us all, ordained and lay people alike, to enjoy the freedom beyond all conditions, a freedom from fears, from gain and loss, from pleasure and pain. This is the joy and happiness of the Buddha.

(Jack Kornfield)

Ajahn Sumedho was ordained in Thailand in 1967 and trained under Ajahn Chah.

ISBN 9780946672233, 1990, 2000, paperback, 148 pages.

Perfect Wisdom: The Short Prajnaparamita Texts
translated by Edward Conze

The Perfection of Wisdom sutras are central to the Mahayana tradition. They offer guidance to those who wish to plumb the depths of their own minds and come face to face with the reality of existence by realising the truth of the Buddha's teachings on Emptiness and Great Wisdom.

Dr Edward Conze (1904-1979) was not only a great Buddhist scholar, but a serious practitioner. His translations are very highly regarded.

ISBN 9780946672288, 1973, 2003, paperback, 284 pages.

The Old Zen Master
by Trevor Leggett

Stories, parables, and examples have been a favoured way of conveying spiritual insights and truths since time immemorial, and Trevor Leggett was a past master at it. He describes this as a freewheeling book: 'I am trying to give a few hints which have helped me and which can be of help to others. Occasionally, a new slant, a new angle or a new illustration — especially if it is an unexpected one — can be a help in absorbing practice, study and devotion.

Trevor Leggett (1914-2000) lived for a considerable time in Japan. He was the head of the BBC Japanese World Service for twenty-four years, was the first foreigner to obtain the sixth dan (senior teachers degree) in judo, and wrote extensively on Zen.

ISBN 9780946672073, 1988, 2011, paperback, 144 pages.

Understanding Karma and Rebirth
by Diana St Ruth

The Buddha saw life as a changing procession of conditions, events, and circumstances, and he recognised that the part of ourselves which is aware, which sees and knows, is never born and never dies. Understanding the cause and effect process and what lies behind it, is the underlying message of this book.

Diana St Ruth is the editor of Buddhism Now online magazine, and has written several books on Buddhism, including *Experience Beyond Thinking*.

ISBN 9780946672301, 2008, paperback, 216 pages.

Fingers and Moons
by Trevor Leggett

The well-known Buddhist phrase 'the finger pointing at the moon' refers to the means and the end, and the possibility of mistaking one for the other.

Trevor Leggett points out that the forms are the methods, but if we forget what the methods are for and they become the goal in their own right, then our progress is liable to stop. 'On the other hand,' he says, 'there are those who say with considerable pride: "I don't want fingers or methods. I want to see the moon directly, directly . . . to see the moon directly . . . no methods or pointing." But in fact they don't see it! It's easy to say.'

ISBN 9780946672073, 1988, 2011, paperback 144 pages.

Find us on line:

www.buddhistpublishing.com

Our online magazine www.buddhismnow.com

Twitter: @Buddhism_now

Facebook.com/BuddhismNow